Walk On

Walk On

Life, Loss, Trust, and Other Realities

John Goldingay

Baker Academic

A Division of Baker Book House Co
Grand Rapids, Michigan 49516

Published by Baker Academic
a division of Baker Book House Company
P.O. Box 6287, Grand Rapids, MI 49516-6287

This volume is a revised and updated version of *To the Usual Suspects*, previously published in 1998 by Paternoster Press.

Printed in the United States of America

Library of Congress Cataloging-in-Publication Data

Goldingay, John.
    Walk on : life, loss, trust, and other realities / John Goldingay.
        p.   cm.
    Includes bibliographical references.
    ISBN 0-8010-2465-X (pbk.)
    1. Christian life. 2. Goldingay, John. 3. Suffering—Religious
aspects—Christianity. 4. Multiple sclerosis—Patients—Family relationships. I. Title.
    BV4501.3.G65 2002
    248.4—dc21   2002018589

Contents

Introduction

I was just fifty-five, we had just married off our younger son, and multiple sclerosis had just deprived my wife, Ann, of the last fragment of her ability to walk when we moved from Nottingham, England, to Los Angeles, California. Ann had once hoped to write something about her experience of the illness, but its progress had eventually made that an impossible project. I had often thought that one day I might write about the way these years had been for both of us, and I suddenly realized that this was the moment. I wrote the first draft during our last weeks in Nottingham and the final version during our first weeks in Southern California. Revising it for this new edition four years later has given me the chance to bring the story up-to-date.

It was partly because of this point of transition in our lives that it seemed the right time to write the book. It was a time for standing back and reflecting. We had lived all our lives in Britain and were moving to the United States. I had been at St. John's Theological College for twenty-seven years and was now moving to Fuller Theological Seminary. I was thus moving from an Anglican seminary of just over one hundred students to a multi-denominational one with thousands of students, and from a faculty of a dozen to a faculty of seventy. I was giving up being principal to return to being a professor. I was leaving a relaxed British setting for a more formal one (no more teaching in a Thirt and shorts). We were giving up a supportive context we knew for a context in which we knew no one.

A few months ago, U2 was coming to town. The greatest rock 'n' roll band was playing the concert of the year. Tickets were hard to find, and a friend and I were discussing how to get hold of some. He proposed driving to the venue in Anaheim at 6:00 in the morning, and I grimaced. "You were keener on the Dixie Chicks, weren't you?" he retorted. It was true. During the four years I have spent in the United States, I have grown to like country music, though not (yet) when sung by men in big hats. It is therefore ironic that the new edition of this book takes its title from a U2 song, which I missed hearing the band perform because I did not want to get up early.

What holds this book together is the experience of walking on with God through the realities of life. Not everything relates directly to Ann and her illness, but one way or another Ann stands within the frame of the whole, sometimes visibly, sometimes invisibly. She drives me back all the time to basic questions about what it means to walk with God. When some other context presses a question, she provides key elements in the subconscious framework within which I think about it.

Admittedly, all I say needs to be footnoted with a warning. We do not understand ourselves completely, and usually anything we say about ourselves has to be taken with a block of salt. It is always wise to assume that there is a lot more iceberg below the surface that we cannot see than there is above the surface that we can see. Further, when people give you the impression that they are being amazingly open about themselves, it is wise to assume that they are being careful to conceal many other things. They are well aware of an invisible iceberg and intend to keep it concealed, at least at the moment. I know that is true of me. But I will tell you most of what I know.

With that warning, I tell you that over the past decade nothing has been more influential in shaping who I am, what I do, what I say, and what I write than my wife, Ann, and coping with her MS and the increasing disability that comes with it. Everything I write is in some sense hers too, even the abstruse academic things, because I would be a different person were I not married to her. I am not the same person I was before the obligation to grapple with Ann's illness grabbed me by the throat.

That does not justify her illness. In a way, it makes it grimmer: Why should I get a bit less immature at her expense? But in other ways it takes the edge off the grimness.

Ann and I met over a boiled egg (well, two) at a Christian students' conference in April 1963. The boiled eggs were soft on the outside and hard on the inside; I have always wondered how they did that. I was wearing my name badge upside down as a way of drawing attention to myself and to my uncooperative instincts. I succeeded, but Ann and I were both involved with other people at the time. Each of us returned to the next year's conference looking for the other.

I had a bad conscience with regard to that previous romance (indeed, I still have), but at least I could claim that I was now uninvolved. Ann could not, which gave her an anxious train journey a few weeks later as she traveled back from the city where her parents lived to London, where she was a medical student. There might have been two young men waiting for her in London. I was the only one who showed up, so I won. Next term I took my final exams for my theology degree; she sent me a red rose each day that week.

Another April day two years later I spent a day with her on the eve of my last term at seminary before I was ordained. It was a warm Sunday evening as we left her apartment with some friends to walk to the underground to get to church. As she crossed the street, she was limping. Good medical student that she was, she made the most alarming diagnosis possible, though she was not histrionic about it. She believed she had disseminated sclerosis, as it was then called. Multiple sclerosis in due course became the normal term as the disease itself became better known. It involves (I expect she told me) a malfunctioning of the nervous system that can affect different parts of the body. Those parts eventually do not respond to messages from the brain because of demyelinizing of the sheathes on the nerves that carry the messages. The next day she walked into the hospital and reported her symptoms and diagnosis. She was treated with due skepticism but by the end of the week was declared right. The next Sunday I hitchhiked to London on another lovely sunny spring day to see her in the hospital. I felt a strange joy and was not at all surprised to get a lift in a sports convertible that took me the hundred miles to London in one go. The medics had started Ann on a course of a cortisone drug whose initials are ACTH and that has something to do with pigs' bladders. This did the trick (how they discovered it would do so I have never known). After a few weeks she was walking normally.

The strange joy I had felt on my way to London came to be associated with three passages from Scripture. One was brought to our attention by Alec Motyer, Ann's rector and before that my inspiration, mentor, and role model as Old Testament theologian. He would want to disown some of my thinking now, but he still loves us. He had gone to see Ann in the hospital and then had written to me, including an allusion to a passage of Scripture that he had been reading that day. It was the story of the wedding at Cana in which one of the guests comments, "You have kept the good wine till last." God does that, Alec commented. It has been an important promise, though not one yet fulfilled except in paradoxical ways.

The other two passages were variations on another point. I wrote them on the flyleaf of Alec's exposition of Philippians, *The Richness of Christ*, which I gave to Ann; they made me weep the day I packed the book as we prepared to move. One passage was from the letter to the Philippians: "for me to live is Christ" (1:21). The other was from Psalm 73, in which someone agonizes about the tough side to life but nevertheless comes to the following realization:

> I am always with you;
>   you hold me by my right hand.
> You guide me with your counsel,
>   and afterward you will take me into glory.
> Whom have I in heaven but you?
>   And earth has nothing I desire besides you.
> My flesh and my heart may fail,
>   but God is the strength of my heart
>   and my portion forever.
>
>   vv. 23–26

Both summoned each of us to make God the one person who counted, so that the other human being whom we loved did not become an idol. It was much easier to mean those words then than it has been to mean them during some of the subsequent years.

The following April Ann had a relapse of the MS, this time affecting her eyes, but again the ACTH did the trick. At the time we were unofficially engaged. I am not sure whether this category of relationship still exists. It meant we were committed to marrying each other, and we believed it was God's will. Our commitment was a semipublic fact, but Ann was not wearing a ring. The reason was that her parents disapproved of me. This was partly because of some aspects of my character (I was not respectful enough or formal enough), but partly because they were very fond of their only daughter and were sad at the prospect of losing her.

During this spell in the hospital, a nurse told Ann that she had no right to get married with an illness like hers, and she certainly had no right to become a mother. The words still haunt Ann and make her wonder whether she did the right thing. In a sense, questions like that are pointless, of course.

A few years ago, we had a peer review and support system for the seminary faculty. Once a year each of us would review the previous year and discuss work and personal issues with two other people. One year things with Ann had evidently been tough, and we had discussed this and talked about how I coped. The then principal's notes of the discussion said something about my nevertheless affirming that I was still glad I had married her. That did not seem quite right. I do not mean that I was not glad but that this was somehow not the framework for thinking about the matter. When you discover that the person you have fallen in love with has an illness such as MS, you cannot then have a solemn discussion about whether you are glad you fell for this person or whether you should terminate the love relationship. At least I could not do that. To ask the question is to deny the reality of what has already happened. It is to deny yourself.

As it happened, my chaplain when I was in seminary had a wife with a chronic illness. One Friday afternoon the summer I learned of Ann's illness he also went as near as he could to inviting me to reconsider whether I wanted to take on what I might be taking on. I think I somehow knew I would understand what he meant only when I was thirty years older, the way you understand your own parents only when you are a parent of teenagers and adults yourself. I also knew that by then it would be too late, or rather that it was already too late. He also knew it was too late, but he still had to say it. And I am glad he did, not because it was of any use to me then, but because it is somehow of use to me now to know that he knew how it would be for me but also that I could not get out of it (I wish I had found a way of telling him this before he died). Relationships lay necessities on you. You cannot go back on the commitment of love without betraying yourself as well as the other person.

I do not know whether that nurse did well to say those words to Ann, those words that came to haunt her. When Ann recalled them to me, as she would from time to time, one thing I would say back is that if she had not married and become a mother, our sons Steven and Mark would not have existed.

Ann and I always say how grateful we are to God that Ann was so well all through Steven's and Mark's childhoods, but I know they were aware of their mother's illness and that they paid a cost in some sense. One year when Mark was seven or eight, Ann had a spell in the hospital, and her mother was staying with us. She made a remark about "when Mommy is better." Mark said quietly, "Mommy will never be really better."

Yes, they have paid a cost. But I would also tell Ann that whatever cost there might have been to them, it has been more than counterbalanced by the positive shaping this experience has had, the sense in which it has contributed to making them who they are. Just recently this was confirmed by our daughter-in-law's account of the caring way our son looked after her during a tricky pregnancy.

Ann and I eventually married six months after that second spell in the hospital during which the nurse issued her rebuke. Within weeks Ann became unexpectedly pregnant. She was on the pill, which was a novelty in the 1960s and was allegedly the innovation that would take the worry and hazard out of sex. The day after we discovered that Ann was indeed pregnant, the *British Medical Journal* carried a report of research suggesting that the particular pill Ann was taking was not as "safe" as some others. We were already in a position to confirm that.

Ann's parents were livid with me. It could not have been worse if we had been unmarried. They had always looked forward to their daughter qualifying as a doctor and coming home to practice, and I had imperiled that, first by marrying her and then by getting her in the family way. But there was a more serious problem. Pregnancy and giving birth are big strains on a person, and stress is a major factor in precipitating relapses of MS. Ann's neurologist (one of her own professors for whom she had great respect) took the view that Ann had no business having a baby within months of a second attack and recommended she have an abortion. It was the end of 1967, the year the Abortion Act had passed in Britain.

We thought and talked and prayed and eventually asked for a second opinion. We went to see another neurologist who put the facts before us to help us make our decision. The decisive comment for me (Ann does not remember this bit) was that though Ann had had two attacks of the illness, he could find no trace of their effects. I did not infer that she had been healed in the sense that she no longer had the illness, but it was enough of a sign that we were to trust God for the future.

The pregnancy proceeded uneventfully, as far as the MS was concerned. Ann had high blood pressure and was in the hospital for some weeks to keep that under control, but this can happen with any pregnancy. One Monday at 3:00 A.M., the hospital called to tell me I had better come now if I wanted to see the action. I remember sitting at traffic lights in North London wondering whether it was really necessary for them to take so long to change at 3:30 in the morning. In those days, it was not customary for husbands to be present at births, but as a medical student Ann had pulled strings. I had always said I did not really believe how babies were born because it seemed implausible. Ann wanted me to see with my own eyes. By 7:45 I was convinced and back at morning prayer in church.

I have a more vivid memory of bringing Ann home from the hospital a few days later. Steven had quite long fingernails at birth and was inclined to scratch himself, so on the way home we had to stop to buy him some mittens. Ann went into the baby clothes shop *and left me on my own, with the baby in the backseat*. What would I do if he woke up? They were the most anxious five minutes of my life, more real in memory than the actual birth.

As Steven has grown to be taller than me, gone to university in the city where I was brought up, taught me how to use a computer, become a systems analyst, married Sue and rejoiced with her in the birth of Daniel and Emma, I have often reflected on the fact that he was supposed to have been flushed down the toilet. I have also come to realize that Steven, and Mark three years later, contributed significantly to the healing of relationships with Ann's parents. Ann thus comments that God's family planning turned out to be wise.

Ann's mother lived for another fifteen years, and I realized near the end how much she and I loved each other. She was a gifted and enthusiastic knitter, and the symbol of her love was making me sweaters, the last of which I wore for her funeral to honor her. (This also gave me the excuse not to wear a suit.) In those last years, it was difficult to believe that we had once so resented each other. All the resentment had melted away, and the thing that had melted it away was having in common the fact that the person we both loved most had a terrible illness. This, too, does not make the illness seem all right, but I have to acknowledge that it is the kind of fruit the illness has had and continues to have.

During the twenty years that followed Ann's first two attacks, from time to time Ann had relapses of the illness, but the medics were able to control it. So during that period she was vice president of the London University Christian Union, qualified as a physician, had two children, brought them up, worked as a community physician and in family planning, and completed postgraduate training in psychiatry, gaining membership in the Royal College of Psychiatrists.

With hindsight, I realize that the pattern of the illness was changing as Ann finished her psychiatric training. She then began further training in psychotherapy, and things started to fall apart. For a variety of reasons, or in a variety of ways, the job and the training did not work. We thought it was partly because her supervisor was not a Christian and was concerned that she might bring God into her work. I thought it might be that she was simply not good at it. I suspect now that the illness was beginning to take away the degree of concentration and insight that this very demanding specialty requires. But that did not occur to me for years. How it felt to me at the time was that she simply had lost interest in *me*. She would come home each day and tell me how grim the day at work had been. I felt I was simply someone to talk to (or at) as soon as the boys had finished their meal. At least that is how I remember it. I feel a bit pathetic about it now, but I know it felt real at the time. I remember how I would wake up in the night and would go downstairs, sit on the settee, and cry out to God in the manner of the Psalms.

Nowadays, students know I enthuse about the Psalms and about the freedom in pain and in joy that they give us. It was new to me then. Once when I was an assistant minister back in the 1960s, the church council was discussing a change in the form of services. I commented that I thought this would be good because it would involve less singing of the Psalms. My rector withered me with a look across the room and said, "My boy, one day you will need the Psalms." The moment had come.

For Ann it was the beginning of a period of years that seem to have been unqualified loss. Instead of having occasional relapses, she began to experience a gradual decline in mobility, self-sufficiency, and other capacities. She needed a stick to walk with, then she could not drive, then she needed a wheelchair. She would forget things, so it was no longer safe for her to work at all. Her retirement due to ill health became effective on the day I became a seminary principal. That seems a cruel coincidence. But at the same time, she then began a new ministry. It was a different ministry from the one some people imagined she might undertake, one that involved counseling or teaching people counseling. It was the inactive but powerful ministry of a person who had once been able to do all that and now could not.

Over the years Ann has been ministered to and prayed for by many high-profile figures on the healing circuit, but it seems that whatever God's intention is for and through Ann, it is to be achieved by not healing her rather than by doing so. The year after she completed her psychiatric training, a John Wimber "Signs and Wonders" team visited a nearby city. I went partly because I wanted to look open-minded. In the course of working through the standard teaching material for such events, the leader told us about his handicapped daughter who had *not* been healed and about how God used her to minister to people, not merely despite her disability but through it. I immediately knew that this was a man who lived in the real world, in the way that I have to. I wanted to believe that God healed and to pray for people's healing, but I also needed to be able to handle it when

God did not heal—not merely to handle it but to make sense of it and perhaps see the other forms of healing in it.

One year we had an unhappy term in the seminary. It seemed to be in some sense my fault as principal for not getting on top of the problem before it felt like a major crisis, and I ended the year convinced that it was time I left, for the seminary's sake and for mine. By the fall it was looking as if I should stay, but I was not feeling that I had recovered from the battering of the preceding year. I imagined the next three terms could only be downhill all the way, because that had usually been the pattern—we spent thirty-odd weeks each year giving out and absorbing problems, and then God restored us over the summer if we were lucky. I say "had usually been the pattern" because that negative patterning did change, and I believe that Ann's influence on the seminary was somehow one of the reasons for this.

I remember a colleague praying with me one day that fall. I was confessing to the fear that although I now knew that this was still the right place to be, I did not think I had the strength to sustain the year. She prayed that the restoring that had been going on would continue abundantly. I remember thinking "fat chance of that," the way you do when someone prays daft things for you. But there is a verse in James about the prayer of a righteous person being powerful in its effects, and over the autumn and winter I could feel my strength continuing to build, which was as well, because there was a lot to think through and handle in the seminary that year.

During the second term, there was a particular week that I knew would be especially busy. It was the beginning of my busiest teaching term of the year. My student group was beginning its period of responsibility for chapel worship. And the Bishops' Inspectors were at the seminary, to satisfy themselves (we trusted) that the seminary was a proper place to train ordinands and to make recommendations about matters we needed to take in hand. To coincide with their visit, we had a meeting of the seminary's governing body to make important decisions about the seminary's future development.

At 3:08 A.M. on the Monday of that week (don't you look at the alarm clock when you wake like that?), I awoke as Ann was having what a neurologist later told me was a tonic-clonic seizure, or rather several of them, in which she first went rigid, then convulsed for some time, then subsided into a daze. In effect, these were epileptic fits, though in Ann's case they resulted from her multiple sclerosis.

As far as I was concerned at the time, they might easily have been the convulsions of someone who was dying. But by 4:30 she was in the University Hospital and by 6:00 was in a bed in its medical admissions ward. She stayed in bed the entire week, hardly moving a limb (voluntarily), and it was not obvious that she was ever going to again. I spent the week commuting between the hospital, the classroom, and the inspectors, rather than just the last two as I had expected. On Friday afternoon I realized that, on the one hand, I was mentally, emotionally, and physically exhausted, but on the other, I was running at one hundred miles per hour and did not know how to stop. The departure of the inspectors removed much of the stress (not that they were difficult—rather the contrary—but the exercise is inevitably a stressful one), and I found myself able to unwind over the weekend. The fact that my spirit made a point of searching out a flu bug a few days later shows that I did not unwind enough. Those events and the story of what happened over the subsequent two years also form a significant part of the background to what follows in this book.

As I have hinted already, not everything that follows relates directly to living with Ann's illness, though everything does so indirectly. The chapters are not a systematic treatment of what it is like to walk on with God—hence, they are arranged in alphabetical order rather than pretending to follow a linear logic. They deal with interrelated questions I have lived with and found myself compelled to think about. Some are questions that have been raised by the experience of living with Ann's illness. Some are questions students have asked. Some have been raised by other aspects of my experience. They are not a collection of questions I would have asked or could have attempted to answer twenty years ago. Perhaps the questions and the answers will look dated in a decade or so. Or perhaps they are questions that are with us always as we deal with life, loss, trust, and other realities.

1

Ascent

I have long puzzled over a particular question about our relationship with God. The Bible seems to assume that this relationship is characterized by love and joy and enthusiasm. At the same time, the great spiritual writers suggest that the development of a relationship with God involves being more and more at home with dryness and darkness, with desert and unknowing. Is there any way of reconciling these two views? I suppose the question interests me partly because I feel that my own life with God has gotten tougher over the years, even over the past week, but also more joyful, even over the past week. And the question more than interests me; it bothers me pastorally, because I see other people whose lives seem to get tougher without becoming more joyful. They become depressed or disillusioned or resentful instead.

What are we to expect as our lives develop? If you have known the joy of being filled with the Holy Spirit, what happens next? Just more of that? If things become tough, does it mean something is wrong? Does God give us nice feelings when we are young and expect us to live tougher lives when we are older? Is it the way people sometimes talk about marriage—the lovey-dovey stuff belongs to the beginning, and as the years go by, you should expect it to grow into something more solid (which is code for something more boring)? I acknowledge I am too much of a romantic to accept that lying down.

It is worth asking these questions because we need to be able to recognize what God is doing with us and to seek what God wants for us. Sometimes people find that the going gets tough and they have no way of looking at how God might be involved when things are tough. This experience can become something you just have to live your way through until it is over, but if that is all you do, it may not produce its fruit.

How can life with God be joyful and tough, tough and joyful? The nearest I have to an answer comes in the form of a story. It is a story that can be interpreted heretically, so have mercy on it at those points.

The Woman of the Mountains

There was a town near the foothills of a mountain range. Living there, you could not help but be aware of the reality of the mountains, though most of the people in the town ignored them much of the time.

There was a woman of the mountains who would visit the town. She brought with her the smell of the mountains, the freshness, the liveliness, the strength, the awesomeness of them. There was a man who was captivated by her, and the two of them fell in love. Their relationship gave him a new kind of acquaintance with the mountains, a new kind of experience of them. It made him more aware of them. He knew that he would never be satisfied until he had climbed them.

One spring day when there were other things to do, she whispered that the time had come, and she took his hand. There was no time to buy mountain boots; he went in the sandals he always wore in spring and summer. They walked hand-in-hand through the outskirts of the town as daffodils came out and children played and men dug their gardens, and he began to realize that he was saying good-bye. Not that he would never see the town again, but he would never see it the same way again. Once he had been to the mountains, it would not be the same town.

On the edge of the town the highway curved away to the left, down the valley toward the coast, but as it began to curve, a dirt road continued straight ahead toward the green and earthy and purple slopes and peaks. The sounds of children and of traffic began to fade, the sound of birds and the smell of grass began to increase, and the sun warmed his back. Each hour they walked, he became more filled with a sense of well-being, happiness, and love. They had their arms around each other's waists, and he could feel the softness of her flesh just above her hip and her fingers on the muscular hardness of his own side. He did not think he had ever been happier, and yet he knew he was only beginning a journey.

After a couple of hours the fields became woods and the dirt road became a path that started to climb. At noon they emerged from the woods to find themselves on a craggy edge from which they could look back over the way they had come. They stopped for a picnic. They talked about the mountains and about the way they had met, about their love and about this journey. And then she said they had to begin walking again. The climb was to become serious.

They were above the tree line now, and the terrain was more rugged. There was still a path; in fact, there were a number of them. He suddenly realized that he could see other figures on these paths—walking a bit desultorily, it must be said. It was not clear where these paths went, and she seemed to ignore them. It was not obvious to him why her route made more sense than the other paths, but he had no alternative but to follow.

And he meant *follow*. Previously, they had walked hand-in-hand. They had strolled, really. Now she led the way. It was partly a practical thing: The way had become narrower, often steep and rocky, and he needed to grab hold of rocks from time to time to help him along. But besides that, she seemed to have become more decisive and dynamic, to have a more specific idea about where she wanted to take him. The playful happiness of the stroll and the picnic seemed to have quite gone. If he thought about it, the odd thing was that he had no less sense of their being together. But he did not have time to think about it much; he was too busy concentrating on the climb, on the difference between safe rocks and loose rocks, on keeping his footing on a particularly narrow ridge. He was surprised that his sandals coped with it all, but they did.

At 3:00 they again stopped for a breather, and again it was a place that gave him a chance to look back to the town and over the way they had come. They had walked for five hours, about four and three-quarters more than he was used to; he was a man who was normally insulated from the countryside by steel, glass, and rubber. The climb since lunch had taken it out of him. It was difficult now to remember the lightheartedness with which they had walked through the suburbs just a few hours ago. They did not talk the way they had when they were strolling rather than climbing or the way they had over lunch. Yet as they sat in silence, he had a strange sense that their awareness of being together was at least as strong. They knew that they were with each other on a crucial journey that was important for her as well as for him. She so much wanted to take him to the top of the mountain where she belonged. It was also becoming difficult to remember the sun on his back. He realized that a mist was descending. It was cold, and as they sat there, he put on his sweater.

Then she hauled him to his feet. She had never done that before. It was again as if the time for words was over for a while. For an instant she looked at him with love in her eyes, then she slapped him on the behind and turned around to begin the walk into the mist. She seemed to know exactly where she was going, though he did not know how. She seemed even more decisive and directed than before, almost a different person from the dancing woman of the mountains who had originally won his heart. But he did not mind. It was like the unveiling of something. This new experience did not take away from what he knew of her before, and what he knew of her before and had fallen in love with made it quite possible to trust this new tougher revelation.

So in a strange way, as he struggled to keep up with her in the mist, he found that the love he felt in his heart was increasing in its wonder, though he did not have time to think too many romantic thoughts. Some of the time he was just wishing he had brought a thicker sweater.

At one point they had to walk along another narrow ridge, and it was a bit scary. He had no idea how far he would go if he fell. Then they had to scrabble up some steep scree, and again he did not like to think about the consequences of losing his footing. Eventually, he had the chance to find out, because he slipped. Like magic she was there, knowing how to make the best use of her weight to enable him to regain his balance. He remembered the story about the two pairs of footsteps becoming one, and he knew that in reality it was a fantasy. He would never be carried (actually, he did not want to be). He would always have to do his own walking, but he would never be alone. And when she smiled at him for a moment as they stood, still a bit precariously, he saw love in her eyes again and realized how much it meant to her that he was making this journey. He loved her back with a new kind of tenderness and commitment and fierceness that he had never felt in his little house back in the town.

In time the mist half cleared, though they could still not see beyond a hundred yards where they were going or where they had been. They had that experience you have with some mountains, when ahead of you rises another ridge and it looks as if it must be the last one, and you think it had better be the last one because you have climbed enough, thank you, and whose silly idea was this anyway, and why are you not playing in the street or digging in the garden? But you climb it, and the reward is— another ridge to face another few hundred yards farther on.

At least now that the slope was more open she could walk alongside him and make a joke or two at his expense, though she would never say whether the next ridge would be the last, and he began to wonder whether she knew or whether this journey contained surprises for her too. But he never stopped trusting her, and he never stopped loving her and thrilling at taking this journey with her and seeing the look of love in her eyes from time to time.

They came over yet another ridge, and just when he had stopped believing it could be the last . . . it was. An extraordinary vista opened before them. The mist was gone, and the sun was shining. They were on top of the world. Once again they could look back on the town from which they had come. They could also look in the opposite direction, and it was an extraordinary scene. They could see the layer of mist below the peak, but beyond the mountains the mist disappeared, and they could gaze as far as the coast. He could see the belt of sand and the sun glinting on the waves.

But his eyes also took in the flat top of the mountain. He suddenly realized that he had not asked where they were to eat or sleep, given that it would be near evening before they reached the summit. He only realized this because as he looked across this little flat mountaintop he saw a picnic laid out: blankets to sit on, a tablecloth, a basket of bread and a bottle of wine, and a man wrestling with a corkscrew.

The woman of the mountains ran to the man and they hugged, and he saw the same twinkle and the same affection in the man's eyes that he loved in the woman's eyes, and he knew this was also his father. He walked up to him shyly but with a kind of confidence that made it possible for them to embrace, because they had her in common and because they knew that they belonged to each other because of the love they shared from her and for her.

The three of them talked about the climb and about the forest and the scree and the mist and the dangerous moments and the falls and the ridges that never seemed to come to an end. But they also talked about the way it was all possible because he and she were together and because of their love for each other and because he trusted her. They ate bread and drank wine and looked in wonder over the vista. They sat in the warm silence of the evening.

They talked about the people in the town who did not know her and the people who did know her but who had never been drawn to climb the mountain. And they talked about the other people they had seen on the mountain. No one had fallen off; there had been no indication of fatal falls. But they had seen people who felt tempted to give up or were on paths that would lead to the top only by a very long way around, people who could not understand why it was such a hard climb, people who had stopped climbing on the sunny lower slopes to pick daisies and enjoy the sun or who had got stuck higher up because they found it all too hard. Each of these people seemed to be walking alone or thought they were walking alone; they did not see themselves as walking with the woman of the mountains.

The two with aching limbs but with love in their eyes agreed
to go and tell them that they did not walk alone and to invite
them to look up and see the love in the eyes of the woman of the
mountains who was walking with them and who mediated and
promised the presence of the one who laid the picnic feast, even
when it did not feel as if he were anywhere near—to invite them
to look and see the love in her eyes that was for them, for you.

I Still Haven't Found What I'm Looking For

Below my notes for that story it says, "Following Christ is a
hard road, but little by little you will see the light in the darkness and drink the water that springs from a dry land." I do not
know where that came from; my friends sometimes add things
to my files when I leave the computer switched on, and so perhaps do other angels, whether it is switched on or not.

In theory, when you come to know Christ, you have found
fulfillment. You have found what you were hungry for. There is
a song by U2 that talks about having climbed the highest mountains so as to be with God, about having run and crawled and
scaled city walls, about having spoken with the tongues of angels
and held the hand of the devil, about believing that Christ broke
the bonds and loosed the chains and carried the cross and all
my shame . . . yet it also declares that nevertheless "I'm still running" because "I still haven't found what I'm looking for."

In terms of spirituality, even when you have found what you
were hungry for, you continue to look forward. St. John of the
Cross, who first made me think about the motif of the mountain because it is prominent in his own writing on spirituality,
also sees us as moving through attraction and engagement to a
marriage relationship with Christ, yet he still speaks of a final
consummation that lies in the future.

U2 were/are high-profile Christians. Van Morrison started off
as a rhythm and blues singer but has sung about mystical experience for over thirty years, since his *Astral Weeks*. His songs
often refer to spiritual guides such as John Donne and William
Blake. He has tried a wide range of religions and had a spell
when he was thought to be a born-again Christian, from which

came the fine 1989 *Avalon Sunset* album (though qualifiedly
commended by the magazine *Q* as "music to fall asleep by a river
by"). It included a duet with Cliff Richard about knowing that
wherever we are, God's light shines on us so that we can reach
out in the deepest of confusion or despair or loneliness and find
God there. But the standout track is the one that gives the album
its title. Van sings a song about the sun setting over Avalon, a
song that keeps asking, "When will I ever learn to live in God?
When will I ever learn?" I now live within a few miles of Avalon.
Only through moving did I discover that it has nothing directly
to do with King Arthur; it is a town on Santa Catalina Island,
off the Southern California coast.

In an interview in the London *Guardian* newspaper, Van Morrison was asked whether he would give up all his musical activity and expression if he could have peace of mind. He said,
unhesitatingly, "Yes."

2

Calamity

A few months before Ann had her seizure, we had been study-ing Job in class. A student who was living with pain of his own asked me what the story of Job meant to me in the context of Ann's illness, and I fell into taking the class through the story of Job in the light of that. I could do it only through tears, because that is the way I am, and the student was weeping his own tears, as were one or two others who had their own pains or who iden-tified with ours. It was the oddest teaching experience of my career. As usual I was teaching with a colleague, and one of the constructive differences between us has always been that she likes to plan everything well ahead and I like to go with the flow. On the way out of class she simply said, "I wish you would tell me when you are going to do something like that" (of course, the problem is that I usually do not know). I cannot remember what I said to the class, and I have no notes, but I expect that what follows bears some resemblance to it.

Testing

Job is the story of a man who had everything but had that everything taken away in one of those calamities that come upon human beings. When Princess Diana and Dodi Fayad died, I was reminded of Job. In some ways, their story is sadder than his. As the television said, they—or at least she—had everything but happiness, and then they lost everything including their lives when they might have been on the verge of finding some happiness together.

The story of Job establishes him as a man who indeed had everything, spiritually as well as materially. He is introduced to us as a whole and upright man who worshiped God and kept well away from wrongdoing. He had the marks of a blessed life: a big family and a prosperous household. He cared deeply about his children's spiritual state.

If you are blessed by God like that, it raises strange questions and puts strange temptations before you. What is the basis of your relationship with God? Do you keep right with God primarily because of what you get out of it? A while ago there was an idea called the prosperity gospel. On the basis of promises in the Old and New Testaments it encouraged us to believe that God intended every committed believer to expect to do well in material ways ("seek first the kingdom of God and all these things will be yours as well"). Job had proven that the prosperity gospel worked. Was he a believer only because of what he got out of it?

And what about God? God was the beneficiary of Job's commitment, worship, and sacrifices. It is rather nice to have someone committed to you, serving you, worshiping you. That raises strange questions about God and puts strange temptations before God. What was the basis of God's relationship with Job? Was Job blessed only for what God could get out of it? Was the arrangement between God and Job a purely collusive contract— you scratch my back and I'll scratch yours? Was it a business contract rather than a personal relationship?

One way to discover whether this is the case is for one party to fail to keep his or her side of the contract. People often assume that our relationship with God is like that. If we slip up in our relationship with God, God is quick to abandon us. Here the question is raised the other way around. What if God abandons Job? The opening scene in the story of Job is a dramatization of that question.

Strange things happen in this scene, and one is not sure how much theology to derive from it. I presume that the story of Job as a whole is based on something that actually happened, but the opening scene takes place in heaven, not on earth. It must issue from human imagination or divine revelation; it cannot be mere ordinary human reporting. The story opens in heaven, where Yahweh sits in court with "the sons of God," the other heavenly beings who participate in making decisions regarding what is to happen in the world and implementing those decisions. They gather to give account of their work. One of them is called the Adversary. The Hebrew word is *satan*, but the word is not someone's name, like the later name Satan. Like the English word *adversary*, it is an ordinary if rare and poetic word for an opponent (an opponent in battle or in court); it occurs a number of times in the Psalms in this connection. It is also used of a heavenly figure in Zechariah 3 and 1 Chronicles 21. Both passages hint at the possibility that the Adversary enters into his work with excessive enthusiasm.

In Job, the Adversary raises the kind of sharp questions that will safeguard against the possibility that the relationship between God and Job is contractual and collusive. In the British Parliament, the opposition party can be referred to as "Her Majesty's loyal opposition." The party serves queen and country by asking pressing questions of the majority party, making sure it does not have too easy a time and making it harder for it to pursue extreme policies. In this scene in heaven, the Adversary fulfills a role that is at once negative and positive. It is negative because of the suspiciousness it presupposes and the trouble it brings, but it is positive because of its potential to vindicate both human beings and God.

The presentation thus differs from the presentation of Satan in some parts of the New Testament, though it is not so different from that in the story of Jesus' testing in the wilderness or Satan's testing of Peter. The nearest I have to an understanding of the relationship between these figures is as follows.

In Revelation, Satan is identified with the serpent in Genesis 3. Now, Genesis 3 offers no hint that the serpent is a supernatural figure. The information that Satan was at work behind the serpent is information that Revelation adds to Genesis. In reading Genesis 3, we need to bring that fact in, but we must not do that too early. We can easily obscure what God meant us to learn from Genesis 3 itself, with its picture of suggestions coming to Eve through an earthly creature with the symbolic attributes of a serpent.

In the same way, the New Testament indicates that the figure of Satan stands behind the figure of the Adversary in Job 1, and in due course, we need to bring that in, but again we must not do that too early. We can easily obscure what God meant us to learn from Job 1 itself, with its portrait of a heavenly being who serves God precisely by asking suspicious questions and proposing drastic testings. It is God, after all, who invites the Adversary to evaluate Job, as it is the Spirit who drives Jesus into the wilderness to be tested by Satan.

If the scene in heaven places some theological pressure on us, the resultant scene on earth places more. Who is this God who allows servants to be killed, animals to be slaughtered, a family to be devastated, a man to suffer terrible illness, and a wife to break down as she watches it, all to prove a theological point? The theological and moral pressure may seem to be reduced if we declare that the scene in heaven and the scene on earth are equally the product of human imagination; they are part of a parable. They are fiction. Yet we may also lose out by appealing to that possibility, for the fact is that employees do lose their lives in the course of doing their jobs, animals are the victims of human greed and natural disasters, and families do get wiped out in terrible accidents. This is not fiction but fact. The question is, How does God relate to those events?

Much of me wishes to disassociate God from them, at least as their cause. I want God to notice when such things happen; I want God to grieve; I want God to comfort; I want God to be able to take the pieces of the shattered jigsaw puzzle and do something with them. But what kind of God would be their cause?

There is a famous conundrum that suggests that the fact of evil indicates that God cannot be both wholly good and wholly sovereign in the world. Either God is wholly responsible for all that happens but not wholly good (which explains the bad things that happen to good people), or God is wholly good but is not in a position to ensure that only good things happen to good people because other beings (including human beings and Satan himself) have power in the world.

My impression is that Christians regularly opt for the second of these solutions to the conundrum. The Job story points to the first solution. Whereas modern Christians prefer a God who is very nice but not very efficient, the Job story offers us a God who does some pretty odd things but who is at least clearly in charge. Even though that raises questions about God's goodness, questions that are the very concerns of the biblical book we are considering, there is some security in it. I am simultaneously frightened and reassured by the fact that God accepts responsibility for the trouble that comes to us, for the disasters to working people and the suffering of animals and the calamities that come upon families and the pain that comes to individuals and the friction that such pain then causes couples.

We are told that the story of Job as it unfolds on earth has a prior history in heaven. By definition this particular history cannot be universalized. Job is a test case. What happens to him happens because he is not like everyone else, because he is not Mr. Average Spirituality. He is Mr. Super Spirituality (as the story will go on to make even clearer). We cannot infer from the explanation of his suffering an explanation of ours. Yet what we may be able to infer is that calamities do have explanations, even if we do not know what they are, for there is another feature of the story of Job that delights me every time I think about it, not least because it establishes a similarity between Job and us. It is that Job himself never knows about chapters 1 and 2 of "his" book. So he goes through his pain the same way we do. And he illustrates how the fact that we do not know what might explain our suffering, what purpose God might have in it, does not constitute the slightest suggestion that the suffering has no explanation. After all, Job could never have dreamt of the explanation of what happened to him.

I cannot imagine the story that makes it okay for God to have made Ann go through what she has been through. But I can imagine that there is such a story. I do not know whether we will ever know what the story is. Job and his wife did not come to know his story, and Job was apparently rebuked for insisting that he should know. Thinking about this now has made me repent again for my periodic attempts to confront God over the question (which work no more for me than they did for Job).

Challenge

"Are you still holding on to your integrity? Curse God and die." One can imagine a little bit of the pain that lies behind Mrs. Job's exhortation, the only words she utters in this story. She is the wife of a man who had everything. And she is a woman who had everything: a successful husband, a fruitful womb, an impressive household, a happy grown-up family. She, too, sees everything collapse. Perhaps she loved Job, and perhaps the two of them could have survived the loss of possessions and even the terrible deaths of their children, but the pain of seeing him physically afflicted was too much. Then she just wanted to end it all, wanted him to end it all. "Curse God and die"—provoke God to send your own thunderbolt.

I may be forgiven for wondering whether in some respects putting up with the pain of someone near you is trickier than putting up with your own. When it is yours, it is yours, and you get on with it. You have the responsibility. The handling of it lies in your hands. When it is someone else's, you are simply helpless, and you may feel guilty too for being unable to do anything.

Job gets on with handling it. His servants are killed and his animals are slaughtered and his children are dead. With almost indecent deliberateness he grieves and he mourns and he kneels, and he praises the name of Yahweh. Physically afflicted from head to toe, he rebukes his wife for expecting that they should receive good from God and not calamity. Who is this man?

Fortunately, he does not exist. In due course he breaks. He will not curse God, as his wife suggests, but he does curse his life. And he begins to ask those questions to which he will not receive answers—even though there are answers he could have been given—questions that all begin with "Why?" They are

"Why?" questions about himself (Why was I not stillborn?), which become generalized into "Why?" questions about people in pain in general (Why is life given to people in misery?).

People's "Why?" questions are sincere, but one suspects that they are not to be taken too literally. I am not sure how much it would have helped Job to have learned about chapters 1 and 2 at this point. I am not clear that he would have responded, "Oh, I see, that's okay then." I have implied that some answers would have been welcome. That is because meaninglessness is difficult to cope with. The fear felt by his friends, to whom we will come shortly, is that everything is meaningless if Job's story is as it looks. Any inadequate answer to the problem of suffering is preferable to the honest and true answer, "We do not know," which is why people go around repeating inadequate answers. They want to reassure us that there is meaning after all.

But Job's problem (and mine) is not just puzzlement but tiredness. When he asks why he was not stillborn, it is not because he wants an answer but because it would mean peace, sleep, rest. When people ask "Why?" we have to ask what the question is behind the question rather than give them an inadequate answer to the question that was in fact not the real question.

I have a strange memory from when I was about thirteen. We used to have to walk a few hundred yards from the school building to the sports pavilion. One afternoon for some reason I undertook to carry everyone's rugby kit from the main building to the pavilion (I cannot remember if there were fifteen or thirty, one team's or two). We all had our kits in drawstring bags, and the players put the strings over my head so that the bags hung down all around me. The thing I remember is the extraordinary feeling of lightness when I took them all off. It was like walking on the moon (except that no one had yet done that).

The memory sometimes comes back to me as a metaphor. For a decade I carried two sets of kits. One was the burden of Ann's illness (it was not really the burden of Ann, of course). It was partly a burden of responsibility. In our house, I had to see that decisions were made and implemented, whether it was what we were to have for dinner or whether we should move to America. In one sense, that was no worse than it is for a single person, though I was having to make decisions for two. It was even more like being a single parent but with the extra dimension that one of the people I was trying to think for was an adult who had an adult's right to be involved in the process.

The other burden was the responsibility of being the principal of a seminary. I could not have asked for a more collaboratively inclined team of colleagues, and I knew that in the end it was God's seminary not mine. But the fact that I was paid more than the rest was a symbol of the fact that humanly speaking there was in the end one person who was humanly responsible for ensuring that the seminary's spiritual life was sound, the courses were good, creative new ideas were generated, and the finances broke even—and that person was me. When I said I was leaving, the child of a student asked if it would therefore cease to be called St. John's Theological College.

Most of the time I did not feel that these responsibilities were a burden. I love Ann, and I love my work. It was when I put the responsibilities down that I realized they were a heavy weight. In 1996, we took a vacation in the French Alps with two friends. Early on we had a late-night conversation that somehow turned into a discussion of whether we looked forward to death. Two of us agreed that it was an attractive prospect because it meant putting down our burdens. It meant we could just lie there. Over the two weeks, however, I forgot about the seminary, and these two friends shared responsibility for Ann, and I realized it was like putting the rugby bags down. I felt lighter, like I was walking on the moon.

Job's cursing and his longing for rest are but the beginning of chapter after chapter of questioning and challenging that dominate his book. They constitute more than one-third of it. Job asks questions, but they are often patently rhetorical—they are questions that conceal statements. "Do I have any power to help myself?" "Does not humanity have hard service on earth?" He expresses longings. "If only my anguish could be weighed." "Oh that God would be willing to let loose his hand and cut me off." He issues challenges, to God as well as to human beings. "Will you never look away from me?" He makes requests, though that is too mild a word. "Tell me what charges you have against me." "Stop frightening me." He makes statements, sometimes as outrageous as the questions and the longings and the challenges and the requests. "If I hold my head high, you stalk me like a lion." "God has wronged me."

The straightness of Job's speech recalls the straightness of the Psalms that pour out human grief, pain, anger, and abandonment, and Job as a whole has been compared to a huge psalm of lament. It is characteristic of those psalms that they display an extraordinary freedom in what they assume we may legitimately say to God, and Job takes that freedom to its logical extreme. There is apparently no limit to what we can say to God. God can take it.

To judge from the end of the book, God does not merely tolerate this questioning but rejoices in it. Another feature of this story that delights me every time I read it is the moment when God comments on the fact that Job has spoken the truth about God, as his friends have not. We have listened to chapter after chapter of Job's storming at God and storming about God, assaulting God and attempting any which way to get God to speak. And we have listened to God put Job in his place. Then we overhear the declaration that Job has actually been speaking the truth about God.

There is a scheme for understanding the way we grow as human beings that moves through orientation, disorientation, and renewed orientation—not once and for all, but on an ongoing basis. Orientation means you know how life works, you know who God is, you know who you are, you know how you and life and God relate. Disorientation is what takes place when that knowledge gets shattered for some reason: Your marriage breaks up or you lose a child or you lose your job or you study theology and discover questions you did not know existed. Renewed orientation involves a fresh understanding that does justice both to your original perspective and to what shattered it. The story of Job takes him through that three-stage process, and the argument between him and his friends is about how to cope with disorientation.

The friends cope with it by denying it, as people often do when they refuse to acknowledge the reality of loss and grief and questions. The friends insist on fitting what has happened to Job into the framework of what they thought they already knew about the way God relates to us and runs the world. In that framework, calamity is intelligible. It respects known parameters. The emphasis of Eliphaz, Bildad, and Zophar, repeated until it annoys us almost as much as it annoys Job and God, is that people who live right in relation to God find blessing, while people who do not experience trouble. When calamity comes, we thus have to ask whether it constitutes chastisement for wrongdoing, as Paul declares is the case with some people at Corinth (see 1 Cor. 11:30). The nuance brought by the angry young man Elihu is that calamity is designed to bring us to repentance for wrongdoing, to draw us back to God, to make it possible for us to grow in our relationship with God. It is related to Paul's understanding of his own experience in 2 Corinthians 12, which Eugene Peterson's *The Message* paraphrases as follows:

> Because of the extravagance of those revelations, and so I wouldn't get a big head, I was given the gift of a handicap to keep me in constant touch with my limitations. . . . At first I didn't think of it as a gift, and begged God to remove it. Three times I did that, and then he told me, "My grace is enough."
>
> vv. 7–9

Another of the delightful features of the story of Job is that his friends are not wrong in living by this theology, as its reappearance in Paul shows. Indeed, Job's own story illustrates this very theology. In the end, the person who lives right in relation to God does find blessing, and the person who experiences calamity is brought to repentance and led on in his or her relationship with God by this experience. That is so by the end. Affirming this is involved in Job's finding the new orientation that also does justice to the old.

But the point of the argument between Job and his friends is to demonstrate that the old orientation does not survive when set against Job's current experience. The friends, or at least Eliphaz, Bildad, and Zophar, will not recognize this. Rather than revise their theology, they rewrite Job's life. In contrast, the reason God commends Job is that Job insists on facing facts rather than hiding from them. Job curses and argues and confronts and challenges and insists and scorns, all in the cause of a resolute requirement that facts be faced rather than evaded. He has lived right by God; what has happened to him does not fit that, and he would like to know how he is supposed to fit that into his universe.

There is a myth about a Greek villain called Procrustes who forced his victims to fit the bed he gave them. If they were too short for it, he stretched them on a rack, if too tall, he cut off the overhang. We may be tempted to make the orientation offered by the story of Job into a Procrustean bed into which everyone's experience must fit, as if the point of the book is to provide the missing piece to the puzzle of suffering: We now have the answer. There are a number of ways of understanding calamity. It may be punishment for wrongdoing (Eliphaz, Bildad, and Zophar), or it may be designed to develop our relationship with God (Elihu), or it may be designed to vindicate our relationship with God (the opening and closing scenes). The question is, Which one applies?

But to ask that question is to miss the point, a point to which attention is drawn by Job's continuing unawareness of what happened in chapters 1 and 2. It is to refuse disorientation. It is to think that we have the problem solved. It reminds me of the preacher who closed his sermon about the Pharisee and the Publican by thanking God that we are not like the Pharisee. We have missed the point. The story of Job suggests that there may sometimes be explanations for calamity that we do not know, but we have to live with God without knowing them.

Trust

Job is a postmodern book. It does not move in linear fashion from the question to the answer. It walks around the question over forty-two chapters, worrying at it, trying out ideas, looking at it from different angles. In one sense, you are no further forward in chapter 42. As I have suggested, it ends up reaffirming the theology that was implicit in its beginning and was explicit on the lips of Eliphaz, Bildad, and Zophar. The great speech in chapters 38–41, with which Yahweh confronts Job, must in some sense be the book's climax, but when I have explained to students how it is the climax, I am not sure I have been convinced by my own explanation.

In that great speech, Yahweh first takes Job on a tour of creation, as if to say, "Are you old enough to have been there when

I created all this, or to have had time in your life to look at all of it? And are you big enough to control it?" Another of the delights of the book (though this time a puzzling one) is that in this pièce de résistance, there is actually little that has not in principle already been said somewhere in the book by Yahweh or by Job or by one of the friends. This tour de force proceeds with huge and relentless power, but that undermines rather than vindicates the submission of Job in 40:1–5. One has the impression that Job surrenders because he is overwhelmed by superior firepower rather than because he is morally or intellectually convinced by an argument. The man who wanted to talk man-to-man with God now wants to get away.

What is the point of God's series of questions? They actually have several points. They begin with whether the world is under control. Job has been challenging God about whether there is order in the world. God challenges Job about whether he is in a position to come to a judgment on such questions. God was there when the world was created and gave it stability, regularity, and order, when potential forces of disorder and death had their bounds and purpose set. Was Job? In his confrontation of God, Job has insisted on arguing on equal terms with God. God's speech is a relentless insistence that Job is too small and the world too big for Job to pretend to be in that position. Job had implied that the world ought to be intelligible in terms that make him the center. God denies Job's self-centered or rather humanity-centered understanding of the world. The world itself is manifestly not exclusively centered on humanity and its needs. So the presupposition of Job's challenge to God is mistaken. The world works the way it does in order to fulfill a broader (we might say, more ecological) agenda, in a sense just to be itself.

Sometimes I find that a long car drive gives me an opportunity to talk things out with God. I am not very good at quiet days and the like, but there is no way of hastening the end of a long drive (well, there is a way, and my friends usually claim that I risk taking it). On a recent car journey I was talking through things with God, and I went on to challenge God about Ann. I said, "You have to have mercy on her." In response, God chillingly echoed back to me my own words, saying, "I will have mercy on whom I have mercy." They are more chilling in their context in Romans 9:15, I think, than when uttered by Moses in

Exodus 33:19. In other words, "What I do with Ann is my business. You can trust me with Ann or not, as you like. It makes little difference to me. It's between me and her, not me and you.
I decline to be held to account to you for Ann." I was being
treated the way Job was treated.

With further irony, once God has Job by the lapels (the reverse
of the stance Job had been looking for), God has no intention
of letting go easily. Job gives in, hoping to escape, but finds that
instead God starts off again; one can almost hear Job's desper-
ate "Oh no!" God's second speech is shorter, but it does seem to
say something new and something quite relevant to my challenge about Ann. Job had been questioning God's fairness, God's
justice. It is the classic question about theodicy, about the justice of God. God's second response is, "Okay, if you are so clever
and so committed to things being fair, you set about running
the world for a while. Put pride down. Dethrone oppression.
Then I will acknowledge you."

"And I am prepared to be evaluated by my own criteria," God
goes on. "I invite you to look at the evidence that I can be trusted
to run the world in a fashion that works things out fairly." God
develops this claim differently than in the first speech. There
God painted on a broad canvas, took Job on a lightning tour.
Here God is David Attenborough on a *Nova* documentary, focusing in a whisper on just two creatures. In Hebrew, they are *behemoth* and *leviathan*. The words could refer to ordinary animals
(ordinary in one sense but extraordinary in another), the hip-
popotamus and the crocodile, the most fearsome creatures you
might ever expect to meet in Palestine. But these words come
to be used for more mythical creatures like the dragon, creatures that symbolize the powers of chaos and disorder that ever
seem to threaten to overwhelm the life of the cosmos and our
individual lives. Set Job alongside either of these creatures, and
if he is wise, he will run a mile. He cannot pretend to control
them.

God's relationship to them is quite different. He is behemoth's
maker, who can approach him with a sword (Job 40:19). He can
treat leviathan as a pet (Job 41:5). God had, after all, specifically
formed leviathan to frolic in the seas (Ps. 104:26). Job knows
about God's relationship with creation and the powers of disorder within it. He is invited to assume that this expresses God's

relationship with the forces of disorder in his life too. That is the only answer he is going to get to the problem of evil. It is the answer he already has. God has demonstrated the capacity to keep the forces of disorder under control. Job has to assume that God is still doing that, even when he cannot see that this is so. He has to trust even when he cannot see.

Job's response, especially in its closing words, is enigmatic. According to the traditional translations, Job says, "I despise myself and repent in dust and ashes." But literally he says, "I despise and repent [change my mind or feel sorry] over dust and ashes." There is no word for "myself" and the preposition means "over" not "in." Since God is about to comment on how truly Job has spoken, the traditional translation seems a poor way to make sense of his laconic words. The context does not suggest that Job needs to repent of anything he has said. Perhaps he is announcing his intention to climb out of the ash heap in the light of the reminders that God has the power and that God makes a commitment to seeing that things work out. Even though he still cannot make theological sense of what has happened, he accepts that he must trust even when he cannot understand, and he determines to do so.

3

Chutzpah

Some while ago I remember being puzzled when I read one or two books about preaching, because they had chapters in them on titles for sermons. I had never felt the need for a title to a sermon. After coming to Pasadena, I think I discovered the answer. A number of local churches advertise not only the times of next Sunday's services but also the subjects of the sermons. It seems to me a wondrous expectation that not only should you have a striking title for the sermon but that you should have it by Wednesday. Both of these I would normally find difficult.

If this were next Sunday's sermon, at last I would be able to fulfill the requirement. This chapter is about "Five Amazing Things That You Can Tell God Not to Do." The subject is partly related to a sermon a colleague of mine once preached about the ten bad habits of God (God is always late, is unpredictable, does not care what people think, has a love that is blind, prefers the broken to the strong, is self-contradictory, does not remember evil and personally repents of evil, is faithful but has changes of mind, is paradoxical, and behaves like a child).

The five amazing things you can tell God not to do are found in a prayer of Moses in Exodus 32. Moses is on top of the mountain with God, receiving instructions about how God and Israel are to relate to each other and what is to be the pattern of worship. At the bottom of the mountain is Israel itself, rather impatient about how long Moses is delaying at the top of this mountain and deciding that it will exercise some creative initiative, indulge in some innovative liturgical development, in connection with how God and Israel will relate and how Israel will worship. Ironically, Israel at the bottom of the mountain is doing exactly the opposite of what God is telling Moses on the top of the mountain. As a result, Moses needs to pray for the people. First, he says, "Don't lose your temper." "Why should your anger burn against your people, whom you brought out of Egypt with great power and a mighty hand?" (v. 11).

It seems strange to think of God getting angry. There are at least two important and precious implications in the fact that God does so. One is that it means God is a real person. God is someone with feelings and passions, such as compassion and mercy. God is someone who loves and cares, who joys and delights, who gets jealous and angry. God is not an abstract entity up there on the top of the mountain or an impassive monarch sitting on a throne in heaven. God is not an idea nor merely the ground of my being. God is a person with passions, and among the passions are anger and wrath. That is part of God's being, in whose image we are made.

It is easy for doctrine to turn God into something we study. God becomes a matter of ideas. We wrestle with understanding the idea of God being one yet also three, and the whole business becomes something abstract. But studying doctrine can also be a way in which we come to understand more about God the person. We can think about God having three ways of being God, all of them ways that relate to us.

Our church in England had a community center, and I remember once discussing the warden's job with her. She knew that as warden she needed to have her finger on what was going on in the community center as a whole and on its policies. She also needed to hang around the various groups so that she was involved and not remote. Of course, she could not do both at once.

God is like and unlike the warden. God needs to have a finger on the world as a whole, but God also needs to be involved with nations, communities, churches, and individuals. God can do both because God is one but has three ways of being God— Father, Son, and Spirit. An old way to think of this (it goes back to the second-century bishop Irenaeus in Lyons, France) is to think of the Son and the Spirit as the two arms of God. One arm was extended at the incarnation, once and for all. The other is extended forever in the world and in the church. The effect of extending two arms, as opposed to none or one, is to make an embrace possible. We are invited by God's two arms to live "in" God—within the embrace of Father, Son, and Spirit. That is what God's being a Trinity makes possible.

God is a person, and the doctrine of the Trinity is designed among other things to safeguard that fact and to show how God can be personal in relation to us. It is not an enigma to be explained but a description to be appreciated. Because God is a person, God also gets angry.

I suspect that the Israelites talked about God being angry because that was often how it seemed to be, to judge from what happened to them. You know when someone is angry with you: If your ear is cuffed, you know there is probably some reason for this. Things go wrong in your life, or in the world, or in the church, and you infer that God must be angry. Then you either try to infer the rational explanation for that and repent, or you conclude that there is no rational explanation, and you say, "Come on, stop it," as Job did.

If we look at the world and the church as we know it, it would be a reasonable inference that God is angry. Perhaps that is why the world and the church (in Europe and North America, at least) are in such a mess. We easily accept the fact that the church is weak and insignificant and shrug our shoulders. Or we make excuses, or criticize the world, or try to do our best, our really pathetic best, to do something about it. Instead, we should ask whether God is angry. Perhaps we should ask God, as Moses does, "Why are you losing your temper?" We might even get a response.

Moses' second challenge to God is, "Don't give up on us. Don't give up on the project that you have begun." "Why should your anger burn against your people, whom you have brought out of

Egypt with great power and a mighty hand?" (v. 11). You have only started the job. You said you were going to take us into the land you promised us. You said you were going to enter into a relationship with us. You said you were going to provide the world with a model of what it was like to be the people of Yahweh. You are not going to give up on the job, are you? You are not going to give up on us, are you? You can't do that.

Again, if we look at the world and the church, where it can seem as if God has given up, then Moses' prayer may be one we should be praying. "Don't give up. The job is only half done, Lord." Moses invites us to challenge God about giving up when the task is only half completed, with regard to the world, the church, and individuals such as ourselves.

Moses' third challenge is, "Don't give the wrong impression." It continues from the second. "Why should the Egyptians say, 'It was with evil intent that [Yahweh] brought them out, to kill them in the mountains and to wipe them off the face of the earth'" (v. 12). "Think of the kind of impression you would convey to the world, to the whole of creation. Think of your own reputation."

This is one of the standard bases on which prayers in the Bible appeal to God. We ask God to do things "for your glory." That might seem a somewhat selfish basis of appeal. It is "for your name's sake," lest people think badly of you. The people in the Bible are unscrupulous in prayer. They will do anything to get God to do the things that are near God's own heart and God's own agenda, to motivate God to act. "You cannot cast us off at this moment and give the impression that you could not do the job after all, that you were not capable of bringing a people into a relationship with you and into their promised land, even if you were capable of bringing them out of Egypt."

And, "Don't be inflexible." "Turn from your fierce anger; relent and do not bring disaster on your people" (v. 12). The Old Testament writers were not afraid of the notion of God having a change of mind. Readers of the Bible worry about this, as if God should not have to do a thing like that. Perhaps part of the explanation for God's willingness to have a change of mind is this: Anyone who is involved in leadership knows that most of the time the decisions you make are not made on the basis that they are 100 percent obviously the right actions, or even 90 percent obviously the right actions. Decisions are often made on a 60-40 basis, if you are lucky, or 51-49. And God is in the same position as anyone else with regard to this. God is always having to choose between the least calamitous courses of action.

So it does not take much to push God from 51 to 49. God had decided to do this but was only a percentage point away from doing the other. "Could you not reconsider the basis on which you have made that decision? Could you not change those figures around? Don't be the kind of person who, once they have made a decision, won't reconsider." Politicians let themselves be caught in a bind in this way, as if changing one's mind is a weakness. Being prepared to change your mind is a strength (well, not if you do it all the time). To be flexible is a strength. And one of the things that is going on in prayer is that we are indeed asking God to do something different from what God was going to do. Indeed, if that is not part of what is going on in prayer, then there is no point to prayer. When we ask God to do things, we are saying to God, "Don't be inflexible. Change your mind. Do something different from what you intended."

Ann and I once invited a friend of ours to come on holiday with us. She declined because she could not afford it, and she did not want to come without paying every penny of her way. The next year she could afford it and came, and we also invited another friend. This second friend seemed likely to decline for the same reason, but our first friend urged us to try to persuade her, not to take no for an answer. I expostulated, "But you wouldn't come last year!" "You didn't try to persuade me," she said. I had given in, taken no for an answer. I would not do it again with her or with God.

Fifth, "Don't forget your word." "Remember your servants Abraham, Isaac and Israel, to whom you swore by your own self: 'I will make your descendants as numerous as the stars in the sky and I will give your descendants all this land I promised them, and it will be their inheritance forever'" (v. 13).

God has made some promises, and Moses is reminding God of these promises. Talk of "claiming" things from God can sound questionable, but there is something to it. You are battering on God's door or on God's chest and saying, "We will not allow you to forget the words that you have uttered to us about your intentions. We will not allow you to forget your promises." When we pray, we can remind God of commitments that God has undertaken, that God cannot get off the hook.

And Yahweh had a change of mind about the disaster that was planned for the people. If we want to be philosophical (in a certain sort of way), of course, we can say that God knew ahead of time that the moment would come for a change of mind and that it was all part of a plan. We may prefer to safeguard God's sovereignty in this way. But the Bible does not do so. More often, the Bible lays the story out as a story, lays it out in narrative form, lays it out as history. It then portrays God's response to Moses as a real response. We are not told, in brackets, "Now, of course, God knew ahead of time that Moses would pray that way, and God had made allowance for that." If this had been so, would God's response really have been a response? In the story the Bible tells, it was a real response. Through prayer God involves us in the process of decision making whereby things happen in the world. It is not the case that God decided by fiat ahead of time, before day six of creation as it were, what was to happen in each of the umpteen years that were to unfold. Rather, God decided to create people who would be made in God's image, with the characteristics of God, and who would then be drawn into the project that God was initiating at the moment of creation. And prayer is one of the ways in which they would be drawn into the fulfillment of that project in the world. That is why, if we do not say things in prayer, things do not happen. Perhaps that is why history has gone on for such a long time. That is why church history has gone on for such a long time. That is why Israel's history went on for such a long time. God never found that anyone suggested the right action at the right moment. God invites us into the fulfillment of the divine purpose for the world. Thus, when people pray, things happen (or are prevented from happening).

So there are five amazing things you can tell God not to do:

- Don't lose your temper.
- Don't give up with the job half done.
- Don't give people the excuse to misjudge you.
- Don't be inflexible.
- Don't forget your promises.

Or to express these five daring exhortations as positives:

- Be patient with us.
- Be persistent with us.
- Be aware of what people think.
- Be prepared to change your mind.
- Be mindful of your promises.

4

Community

When people asked me what I thought we would miss in moving to the United States, they often commented on the difficulty of leaving a place where you have lived for twenty-seven years. Neither the geographical place nor the length of time seemed particular issues for me, and Pasadena soon became home. I did expect to miss working, living, and worshiping in the kind of community to which I had belonged—I would have missed the community even if we had been there for only five years. I knew I would especially miss it because it had been such a supportive context for Ann and me as we lived with Ann's illness, all the more so with the particular pressures of the last few years.

From time to time I have heard people complain that a seminary is not a community—they do the same at Fuller. They say this in anger and in anguish. At St. John's I think I heard it less in our latter years, and that in part has something to do with Ann, with the role she played in focusing the community for some people. Indeed, there is a significant contrast between that protest and the contents of the following note a student wrote to me when (unbeknown to him) we were in the midst of wondering whether it was time to leave.

> For the last five or six weeks I have been praying for you. I think this has come from my struggling with questions about what community is. My conclusions are that there is a huge pressure from secular society's values on seminaries, which can cause conflict for the community and therefore conflict for you. The Church (as an institution) is affected by these values and therefore unwittingly demands some of them be part of our seminary—i.e., more authority and stratification etc.—therefore putting more demands on you. Even my own presuppositions and insecurities want these values, when I am not close to God.
>
> I therefore would like to say that I feel we are living as a biblical community, i.e., a type of corporate prophecy. The balance we have to have here is that we do not lose the secular part of ourselves but struggle and transform it by the openness of our community. We students feel we can be honest and not judged. If we can be honest, we can live in truth.
>
> I also realize that with a prophetic community goes rejection, uncertainty, and a desert. Perhaps this is why I feel I need to pray for you.

As I have implied, I did not feel that kind of pressure anywhere near as much as I once did, and I suspect that Ann is the key to that. But the student is right that there is a strong tension within many of us between a desire for a oneness in Christ that denies hierarchies and a desire for the security of having somebody in charge who will exercise strong leadership. He is also right that the former is God's ideal vision for the church (and the world, for that matter). I confess that I worry a bit about people who are quite willing to carry the burden of leadership forever, who are even enthusiastic about it. Jotham's parable in Judges 9 wisely reminds us that the best leaders are probably not the people who want the job.

Marks of Community

Being able to utter the complaint that a seminary is not a community presupposes various things: that we know what a com-

munity is, that a seminary ought to be one, and that this is important. The second and third of those I believe. The first assumption, that we know what a community is, is trickier.

A few years ago a sociology professor told me about some
research that had been done regarding the essence of community, the nature of community, the real meaning of the word.
The researchers discovered only that it was a "warm" word, it
suggested something nice. Of course, that was underlying the
anguish that resulted when people said a seminary was not a
community. They were saying seminaries were cold. It also
explains the degree to which the word community is used. In a
political context, for instance, we talk about the local community and community tax and the European Community and the
international community and the community of faiths and even
the world community. It is a word with such a wide range of
meanings that to say that a church or a seminary or an area is
a community, or that it is not, is nonsense until we have said
what we mean by the word in this context. Ever since hearing
of that research I have avoided using the word and have felt no
deprivation; avoiding clichés is usually an aid to clear thinking.
How can we begin to define community?

Psalm 111 (RSV) gives us some of the markers of a community. Not surprisingly, the first feature of community life that it
points to is worship. It is a psalm, so that would be so, would it
not? But some psalms begin in other ways, so maybe it is worth
noting that this one begins with worship. "Praise the LORD," it
starts. The verb is plural. Praise is something the psalm challenges people to do together. But then immediately it changes
to the singular: "I will give thanks to the LORD with my whole
heart." Then straightaway that individual worship is once more
set in the context of the community: "I will give thanks to the
LORD . . . in the company of the upright, in the congregation"
(v. 1). The psalmist believes that the deeply felt worship of the
individual is important, but in the way the sentence works, that
individual worship is set in the context of the worship of the
community.

might suggest various insights. It might hint that
valuate the full significance of our individual wor-
we can see how it feeds into corporate worship. It

might also hint that the reality of corporate worship depends on the reality of individuals worshiping at the heart of it.

This psalm points us to worship as the first feature of the community to which the psalmist belongs. Worship is not what people spend most of their time doing, even in a convent. But worship is the framework, the heart, and the key to what the church is and does as a community.

The second feature of community that we hear of in Psalm 111 is study. As is the case with worship, that clearly fits the kind of community I have belonged to, but significantly the psalm implies that it also fits other kinds of community. "Great are the works of the LORD, studied by all who have pleasure in them" (v. 2). Maybe that has already been hinted at in verse 1, when the psalmist speaks of worshiping with the whole heart, because in the Bible the heart is not just the center of emotions. In fact, if you want to talk biblically about your emotions, you are as likely to speak in terms of your stomach or your kidneys ("Darling, I love you with all my kidneys"). The heart is the center of the whole person as a thinker and not just as someone with feelings. It is the locus of the mind. The worship that the psalm speaks of, therefore, is one that occupies the psalmist's whole mind. "I will praise the LORD with my whole mind." It is exactly the determination Paul urges on the Corinthians (see 1 Cor. 14:15).

In the common life of a seminary, the feeding of the mind probably occupies more time than any other occupation apart from sleep. Sometimes the two coincide, of course. In a fellowship group, we were once asked to think of the word that best described our life at that moment. One person wrote "a sponge." That summed it up rather vividly. Come to the worship of the community, says the psalmist, and squeeze your sponge out to the glory of God, make it material for praise, pour it all out to God, and then go and fill it some more. "I will praise the LORD with my whole mind."

"Great are the works of the LORD, studied by all who have pleasure in them." The works are the great acts that God has done in Israel's story. The psalm goes on to recall the way God brought the people out of Egypt, the way God was revealed to them at Sinai, the way they knew God's provision in the wilderness, the way God gave them the land of Canaan. "Great are the

works of the LORD, studied by all who have pleasure in them."
One reason people study theology is that they have become
people who take delight in what God has done. Yes, indeed,
says the psalm, the logical consequence is that you will want
to study what God has done. The Prayer Book version says that
these works of God are "sought out" by those who have pleasure in them, and that is the basic meaning of the verb. If you
go looking for something you need, this is a word you could
use. To study is to ask hard questions about something that
matters.

Once again it is a plural word. The psalm is talking about a
community matter. It presupposes the engagement of my whole
mind, but it also presupposes that my study takes place in community. Over recent centuries higher education has become a
rather individual matter. It is a process whereby I write my
papers and take my exams so that I can get my degree. In Jerusalem, I have seen Jewish people studying the Torah together,
and it is a very different activity. People sit in little groups, the
whole person engaged, intent, fingers wagging, living out the
conviction that studying Scripture is a corporate enterprise and
that a body is never more alive than when its members are studying Scripture.

The psalm presupposes that people were enthusing over the
great acts of God that made the people of God what they were.
When did they do that? Commentators often reckon that a psalm
like this belongs at a festival such as Passover or Tabernacles,
when Israel especially remembered the great acts of God. The
essence of those festivals was that they were occasions when
people gathered together and lived together as a community.

That gives me the excuse to include a third feature of the
nature of a community, the element of common life. There is
something special about time spent living with other Christians
and focusing on the faith together.

There is something else about celebrating the great acts of
God. It was not just a matter of recalling what God had done
centuries ago. Events were celebrated with the assumption that
they were still having an effect now, that they had started a
process that was still under way, even that they had established
a pattern that could be repeated. There may be a more explicit
hint of this in the phrase, "I will give thanks to the LORD with

my whole heart." The verb is the word you would usually use in giving thanks for something God has done for you personally. It is the word for giving your testimony. The celebrating relates to new events, not just old ones.

In other words, to talk about giving thanks to God presupposes that you have gone through some tough experience and that God has brought you out the other side—it is for this that you are giving thanks to God. And in this psalm, that is a community experience. Community involves having your own experience of being rescued from oppression, sustained in the wilderness, committed to the covenant, and taken to the edge of the Promised Land. It implies not just individual experiences of those things but experiences of them that people share with each other.

I once read a fascinating article about liturgy, justice, and tears, about bringing our own suffering and the suffering of others into worship. The psalms are very good at that, of course. The article talked about a service in South Africa during apartheid in which people brought not only bread and wine to the communion table but also a set of chains and a rubber bullet and a passbook. They brought their suffering into worship, into the very service that focuses on the suffering of the crucified God. That belonged to the essence of their life as a community. I have no doubt that it brought them together as a community. I have seen that happen myself when people have grieved before God together.

Bringing suffering into worship is usually difficult to do for at least two reasons. One is the cost to the sufferer, for to talk about our suffering before God implies talking about it to ourselves, coming to terms with it. The other reason is theological. It is Job's friends' problem. We are not sure the faith can cope with it, whether it really has the answers, whether God really knows about suffering. With our heads we know that God does, but in our hurt hearts we are less certain, and we are not sure we can risk asking the question. In a community, we owe it to each other to allow people to give voice to the grief, hurt, and pain of the people of God and of the world. When we do that we will find we are a community in grief, a community in prayer. We will then find that one way or another the God of the signs and wonders of the exodus, of the wilderness, and of the Promised Land will be our God. We will find we are a community in wonder at what God does in our midst, a community in answered prayer, a community in testimony that occupies the whole heart and mind.

There is one other feature of community life that I notice in Psalm 111: obedience. The Israelites were a people who lived by Yahweh's precepts and knew that those precepts were a reliable guide for life (v. 7). They were a people who lived by the covenant that Yahweh had ordained forever (v. 9). They knew that the fear of Yahweh, reverence before Yahweh, awe before Yahweh, and obedience to Yahweh were the keys to wisdom, the keys to understanding (v. 10). Only insofar as they were a community in obedience would all the other things be true. Their worship would not count for anything otherwise. Their study of God's acts would not count for anything; it would not lead to real wisdom, only to knowledge. Their common life would be imperiled if there was no obedience.

Obedience in what respect? Jesus once said that the heart of the Torah, which the psalm commits itself to, was love for God and love for one's neighbor. When he was asked to explain it a bit more, he told a strange story about a man who got mugged and was ignored by the people who were committed to obedience but received neighborly treatment from an unexpected source. So the question is, What would it be like to be a community of obedience in love, a community that did not just sing about the servant King but itself comprised a servant community?

Resourcing and Resourced by a Community

On the occasion of Ann's seizure, one of the Bishops' Inspectors commented that it was bound to make a big difference to the seminary having the principal's wife taken off to the hospital like that. I was a bit surprised or puzzled. The comment made me think more about whether the fact that the principal's wife had an illness made a difference to the seminary all the time. There were a number of reasons why I would periodically think that I had no reason to be the principal. One of them was that I could not do certain things because of Ann. There were ways in which being committed to Ann held me back or occupied my time or grieved my heart. But then I told myself that the other side to that coin, the positive aspect, was what Ann brought to seminary.

As well as contributing to my making, she contributed to the making of the students. I have a hunch that long after anything I have ever said about the Old Testament, about which I care so passionately, has disappeared from most people's memories, some aspect of the memory of Ann will abide with them. In some way they have been shaped by her, as I have been shaped and as our sons have been shaped. I also have the suspicion that she formed part of the identity of that community. The fact that she was the principal's wife determined something of its nature and even contributed significantly to its growth in health and maturity.

Theological ethicist Stanley Hauerwas has written among other things about Christian understandings of suffering and medicine and mental retardation. In a book called *Naming the Silences*, Hauerwas asks what we mean by "pointless suffering" and suggests that it means "we cannot situate this life with its suffering in any ongoing story carried by a community that can make this suffering person's life its own."[1] That draws attention both to the deepest problem about Ann's illness and to the most positive aspect of its mystery. The deepest problem is that God achieves so much through that illness, perhaps much more than God achieves through my ministry, but that this achievement comes about through a systematic ignoring of what seems best for Ann, through a systematic withdrawing of so much that she has valued (her work, her independence, her mobility, her intellectual ability), so that she is reduced to a person who sits in her chair unable to remember what day it is. And yet the edge is taken off the awfulness of that insofar as her life is situated in and her story is carried by this community that makes her life of loss its own and shares its love with her.

Hauerwas goes on:

Historically speaking, Christians have not had a "solution" to the problem of evil. Rather, they have had a community of care that has made it possible for them to absorb the destructive terror of evil that constantly threatens to destroy all human relations.[2]

The community has shared its love with her and has shared its love with me. I recall some years ago puzzling over Romans 5:5 for quite a long period, worrying at it like a dog with a bone. "Hope does not disappoint us, because God has poured out his love into our hearts by the Holy Spirit, whom he has given us." What does that mean? Not, What do the words mean? but, What reality are they referring to? I wondered whether there was some charismatic outpouring of God's love that I had not had and might seek from God. And yet perhaps one reason I stopped fretting over the question was that such an outpouring as I might long for sounded rather frothy and triumphalistic. Even if God had indeed overwhelmed me with an awareness of love, I cannot see how I could have fitted it in with how Ann was. I had no doubt of God's love for me and no difficulty expressing my love for God, but I felt that experience of God for me had to be experience of felt mystery more than felt love.

That changed over those weeks that followed Ann's seizure, when I came to feel overwhelmed by love in a way I never had been before, but in a way that recognized hurt rather than ignored it. In another book called *Suffering Presence*, Stanley Hauerwas suggests that no matter how sympathetic people may be when we suffer, "no matter how much they may try to be with and comfort us, we know they do not want to experience our pain."[3] It is a difficulty heightened and prolonged by chronic illness, which alienates sufferer and family from other people. So we deny our pain and pretend and thereby increase our loneliness.[4] The comment provides a clue to the question as to why Christian communities often hide their pain from each other. "We know," says Hauerwas, that other people "do not want to experience our pain."[5]

We think we know. What I find odd about his comment is that it is at the same time deeply illuminating and deeply wrong, sharply contradicted by my experience (by his, too, in practice, I discovered from correspondence with him). It was precisely the pain I felt that made many seminary people reach out to me as well as to Ann after her seizure and made others grieve the more because they could not think of a way of reaching out to me, short of bringing me seminary food when I had the flu, which was a paradoxical form of showing love, I thought.

Some were people who reached out to me because of the love that God had put in their hearts, and that disproves Hauerwas's dictum one way. Others reached out to me with the love that God inspired because of a particular reason, because of the pain in their own hearts.

One Thursday we had been praying for people in chapel, and a student who was going through a particular experience of pain went forward to ask people to pray. I found myself not moving out to pray with him but staying in my place, crying. A well-meaning brother came to pray with me, and I had to explain that I did not think I was weeping for myself this time but for that student.

That term I looked in the eyes of the people who came to sit with me and saw the hurt that gave them access to mine, and it was often then that I felt overwhelmed by love, overwhelmed by the love of human beings, whose real fleshly human love it was, but who were also vehicles of the love of God. And I said one day through my own tears to someone whose pain I knew and which I could at that very moment see in their eyes as they simultaneously hurt for me—I said that it was not fair that they should be supporting me when they had hurt in their own hearts. But even as I said it I knew it was nonsense, dangerous nonsense at that. I was trying to make their own hurt pointless. They were instinctively letting their own pain bear its terrible fruit in their capacity to love me.

I thought, "Well, if God could not create a world from which grief was absent, at least God has created a world in which this grief bears fruit rather than returning to earth having borne nothing." The fact that the overwhelming of God's love took place through the tears of people's grief made it possible to bring together Romans 5 and the fact of pain in a way that is actually true to Paul, for he himself brings suffering and love together.

But why bring God in? Was this not just human love, and none the worse for that?

One evening I went to bed straight after eating my dinner because I was miserable and I could not think of anything else to do. But unfortunately, I was not tired and could not get to sleep, so I just lay there feeling more and more miserable. I longed to have someone put their arms around me. I know I could have gotten up and gone to see someone, but perhaps I was thinking about whether this was all too exclusively human, about whether God was just an extra level of interpretation I was putting onto human caring (and risking dishonoring it in its humanity). I cried out to God, "I know you care, but your arms cannot be felt as a human being's can." And then it was as if physical arms were around me, and I felt embraced by God as I had never felt before. I could sleep the sleep of the cared for.

I realized that there had been a particular sort of embrace that I had valued and subconsciously sought over previous weeks; not the regular sort of hug when you stand man-to-man, but a kind of hug that involved someone standing over me and seeming bigger than me, so that their embrace shielded me from the world and the future and my anxieties and life's demands. At the end of the Blessing of Moses in Deuteronomy 33 is the promise that underneath are the everlasting arms. But at the beginning of the Song of Moses in Deuteronomy 32 is the promise that God is a mother hen fluttering over its young. It is that sense of being covered and protected that I have so valued as people have incarnated the protecting love of God to me. I was reminded, too, of Ruth's plea to Boaz to "cover her" with the wings of his garments, as it were, and of Bruce Springsteen's wonderful song "Cover Me."

Oddly, as well as reassuring me that God was real and not just an interpretation of human love, that supernatural experience of God's embrace gave extra value to the human love. Usually, God had been reaching me through other people. Now I had more conviction that it was God who was caring for me, but that usually God chose to do so through other people. Why?

I came to recognize that there were reasons peculiar to me and related to what God wanted to do with me. I do not think that in life in general I deny my pain, but I recognized that I had subconsciously felt I had to live with it alone. Perhaps I had assumed that there was a grief in Ann's illness that was peculiar to me and I had to live with it alone. I would do so in the evening, for instance, after she had gone to bed. I am not sure that doing so is wrong (though it may be). But whether it is right or wrong, paradoxically, the experience of that bout of Ann's illness made me face my loneliness, which I think I had barely owned.

But there is also a theological reason for God's choosing to reach out to us through each other: Love is sacramental. We are physical people, and the physical embrace we offer each other is a sacrament of the embrace of God. God can feed us spiritually without bread and wine, but bread and wine is the normal way, because we are fleshly people. God can embrace us directly and not use other people, but using other people is the normal way, because we are fleshly people. People who hugged me in such a way as to make me feel protected became sacraments of the protectiveness of God.

There were one or two interesting characteristics about the people who became sacraments to me like that. Many of them had their own hurt. Many of them were also nearly half my age. It reminded me of the way God delights to use the younger rather than the elder child in Genesis, and I wonder whether it models the turning upside down of expectations that may be true of the gospel. It also reminded me of something I had failed to convince the seminary about during the previous year, that we had within that community the pastoral resources to care for each other.

In the meeting between the Bishops' Inspectors and the college's governing body, to which I referred in the introduction, we fell into a discussion about the nature of community in a seminary nowadays. One of the inspectors wondered aloud whether the loss of the old markers of a seminary—everybody in chapel morning and evening, everybody eating all their meals together, and so on—would eventually mean the loss of any sense of community. Two governors who were students twenty years ago responded with one voice and enabled me to see something that I had half seen but had not quite articulated to myself. The old markers of a residential seminary had actually disappeared a quarter of a century ago. If we had been living on the capital of the past, we would already have been bankrupt.

The reality of the seminary community, which was always recognized by people who came in from outside, whether for an hour or a day or a week or a month, had little to do with whether people were all on parade at particular moments (as is just as well, because we were an individualistic lot who made our own decisions about whether to be on parade for anything). It was a reality in lots of little groups, networks, twos and threes and fours, some of which I never knew existed until those painful few weeks. And it was a reality in the way in which those groups were not closed, self-indulgent cliques but a crisscrossing network, so that the seminary was more like a church than it had ever been. In fact, it was modeling (the two governors argued in unison) a realistic, viable vision of community for parish life. As the opposite of closed, self-indulgent cliques, these groups were a network open to a man in need, not requiring him to force his way into them (for he lacked the confidence to do that) but on their own initiative opening their arms to him and daring him turn away. The church, says Hauerwas, is a company of people who have learned how to be ill and to ask for help and how to be present to one another in and out of pain.[6]

One of the students said to me one day that term, "It isn't going to be the same again, you know," and the words strangely upset me. It was partly because I was at that stage of the flu when you get overwhelmed by waves of moroseness and gloom, but it was partly because they were strangely pregnant words, real prophetic words, words whose significance I have kept pondering. Did he mean it wasn't going to be the same for Ann physically—was she ever going to be the same? Did he mean it wasn't going to be the same because once you have had that kind of experience you can never relax again? We may laugh again, but we will never be young again? Certainly, I could not contemplate jaunts with Ann halfway around the world to the Middle East or South Africa or somewhere anymore (but here I am taking her to the United States!). And if Ann did become as mobile as she had been before, what would be the point? Something like that seizure would happen again one day, or something else quite different, so what was the point of going through it and coping with it and recovering from it when you were going to have to go through it again in some other form?

Or did the words mean that the way people related to me would never be the same and that I would never be the same? One day I said to God that presumably now we could get back to normal, which would mean I would cease belonging to those networks of relationships and I would have to be alone again. I half expected God to say, "Don't be stupid," because that is what God often says to me. Instead, God said yes, at which I was a bit taken aback. God did nuance the toughness of the yes by promising me that there would be people who would reach out to me but that I would have to receive them for what they are and who they are and live with the insecurity of that.

It turns out that thirty or forty days in the wilderness and being ministered to by angels may be simultaneous experiences rather than sequential ones. In the wilderness, God ministers to you through people in miraculous ways. Stone is turned into bread by the word that comes from the mouth of God. But by definition that is an experience you have to let God stay in charge of. It is not even covenanted. You have to accept the angelic ministry as it comes, in the form in which it comes, and live from day to day, from loaf to loaf, from hand reaching out to hand reaching out—and live through the times when there are no angels or loaves or hands. If being overwhelmed by love is the fruit of the Holy Spirit, then it is presumably bound to be a temporary rather than a permanent experience in this age, because that is the nature of the Holy Spirit's work. Jesus' experience repeats Job's in illustrating the way the Adversary sometimes has the power—under God—to take us into what looks like God-forsaken wildernesses. The Spirit gives us foretastes of what heaven is like, but they are foretastes, which in this age remain incomplete and are designed to provide guarantees and to provoke yearning. On the other hand, you also have to be wary of failing to recognize angels and loaves and hands, insisting that all you see are stones when God is doing those miracles of provision for you—at least, I have to be wary of that. For it is true that "hope does not disappoint us, because God has poured out his love into our hearts by the Holy Spirit, whom he has given us" (Rom. 5:5).

Darkness

"The LORD is my light and my salvation." So Psalm 27 begins. Without God, therefore, apparently I lack light and salvation. What I experience is darkness and loss, gloom and calamity, night and disaster, autumn bringing winter, and decline bringing death.

Someone was talking to me a year or two ago about the way gloom descended upon her as winter drew on and about a suspicion that this mirrored the literal gloom of winter. Perhaps the darkness of winter makes it harder for us to escape the inner gloom of our own hearts.

A few weeks after Ann's seizure, when life was beginning to get back to normal, a friend asked whether it was time I talked about the implications of the experience for me personally, about the broader implications of coping with Ann's illness and how I felt about them. I had in fact wondered about that myself, so I surprised her with a positive response. I got in touch with a former student who is a hospital chaplain and has a counseling ministry and went to see him half a dozen times. The visits were extremely useful, and some of the thoughts I have attempted to

express in this book emerged in those sessions. The possibility
that the darkness of winter makes it harder for us to escape the
inner gloom of our own hearts reminds me now of something
that happened in one of those visits.

On that occasion I cried as I attempted to articulate something that was actually positive and hopeful. This crying at an
illogical moment had already happened once or twice, and I was
quite angry about it. I wanted to know why it happened. The
counselor was the type who would usually say nothing and turn
the question back on me (which usually worked), but this time
he responded. He suggested that articulating hope and facing
darkness, gloom, and pain were close to each other, because the
hopeful statement was a denial of the gloom that I was inclined
to feel. Joy and pain are next door to each other. Inside me are
dark corners where the gospel has not yet had its way, places
where I do not really believe there is gospel, places where all is
gloom and winter.

That in turn reminds me of a Friday in November when as a
seminary community we sought to wait on God together. People talked of the dying autumns of their own lives that mirrored
the autumn of nature. And it was only November! "How will we
face January and February?" I asked myself. Sometimes January and February are tough times in a seminary, as in churches,
and one reason is that we cannot face the January and February, the gloom, despondency, and darkness in our own spirits.
We repress them, and they come out in ways that evade the pain
but destroy the potential for growth that they contain. It is with
regard to these, among other things, that Psalm 27 invites me
to say, "The Lord is my light and my salvation."

In that sharing in November, I remember feeling downcast
at the thought that for me the stripping of leaves seemed to be
a perpetual experience, as if autumn never ends and spring never
comes. But someone pointed out to me that this is where the
illustration breaks down, because stripping in itself turns out to
be fruit-bearing. Later I came across the following quotation
from John Donne, from a sermon on Christmas Day 1624 (no
trivial sermons on Christmas Day in the seventeenth century!):

> God hath made no decree to distinguish the seasons of his mer-
> cies; in paradise, the fruits were ripe the first minute, and in

heaven it is always autumn, his mercies are ever in their maturity. We ask . . . our daily bread, and God never says you should have come yesterday, he never says, you must again tomorrow, but today if you will hear his voice, today he will hear you. If some king of the earth have so large an extent of dominion, in north and south, as that he hath winter and summer together in his dominions, much more hath God mercy and judgement together: he brought light out of darkness, not out of a lesser light; he can bring thy summer out of winter, though thou have no spring; though in the ways of fortune, or understanding, or conscience, thou have been benighted till now, wintered and frozen, clouded and eclipsed, damped and benumbed, smothered and stupefied till now, now God comes to thee, not as the dawning of the day, not as in the bud of the spring, but as the sun at noon to illustrate all shadows, as the sheaves in harvest, to fill all penuries. All occasions invite his mercies, and all times are his seasons.[1]

Donne did not know that in Israel itself you can move from snowy winter to desert sun within an hour. (I dare say you can do the same in California, but I stay within reach of the beach myself.)

That in turn reminds me of the carol "When the Green Blade Riseth":

> When our hearts are wintry, grieving, or in pain,
> Thy touch can bring them back to life again.

"The LORD is my light and my salvation—whom shall I fear?" the psalm goes on. "Of whom shall I be afraid?" In one sense, I do not fear. I do not get afraid. It's not a virtue or anything; I just have that bit missing, like embarrassment. Once on a seminary trip to Israel we were driving a minibus through a village near Hebron and people started throwing rocks at the vehicle. It seemed that something very nasty could happen, and I was in the navigator's seat, in the front line for getting hurt if it did. I remember thinking, "This is an interesting experience, but it will be good when we are out of here." I also remember realizing afterward that I had not exactly felt afraid, as some people had. (One of my colleagues will probably never forgive me for that piece of mis-navigation.)

On the other hand, I do get anxious, which is different but related. I can worry. I can wish there was somewhere to hide or that there was someone to hide me, to protect me.

And the psalm dares me to say, "The LORD is the stronghold of my life—of whom shall I be afraid?" There are women's refuges where the one thing you can be sure of is that there will be no men there, nobody to be the life-threatener that your husband or your lover or your pimp could otherwise be. They are places where you can begin to learn to relax and regain the strength to face life.

Which takes us into seeking, for that is where it takes the psalmist in offering his testimony. "One thing I ask of the LORD, this is what I seek" (v. 4). One of my colleagues once described someone as a "focused" person. It made me think about the idea of being unfocused, about what that involves. I take it to mean something like this. You can be a person who does all sorts of things, but they are a bit like grapeshot. There is no unity to them, no one aim that holds them together. You are all over the place, easily distracted from one thing to another. That is key to the idea, I think. But lying behind it is the idea that there is no center to what you are and do. There is no "one thing."

I find it interesting that Psalm 27 talks about focusing on one thing in the context of talking about darkness. It reminds me of John of the Cross, the person from whom we get the phrase "the dark night of the soul." John was an interesting person, a Spanish theologian and mystic in the sixteenth century. I had always thought of him as rather remote until I discovered that he had a job rather like mine. He was the principal of a community, trying to get a grip on the students and keep the church authorities happy and write the odd book.

One piece of bad news I discovered is that in *The Dark Night* he talks about two dark nights of the soul. There is one that is self-imposed as well as one that is God-imposed. The first involves our committing ourselves to a life of denial in order to find the real light in God, except that John talks about it as finding the real darkness in God. Paradoxically, the light of God is so bright that when it really shines on us it blinds us, it puts us into darkness.

When John talks about the dark night, he talks about it in terms of stripping away the things that do not really matter to us. The dark night takes us back to basics. It raises the question of who we really are and what we are really aiming at. John of the Cross sees it as a virtue that darkness, stripping, takes us back to basics, makes us concentrate on what deserves concentration. "There is one thing I do: I am going for a target," says Paul. "There is one thing you lack," says Jesus to a young man with many possessions. "There is only one thing that is needed," he says to a woman worrying about the dinner. "There is one thing I know: I can see now," says the man born blind. "There is one thing I have asked of the LORD," says the psalm, "one thing."

If we are in the dark at the moment, or if we find ourselves walking in the dark in due course, John says, we need to let it strip us, let it focus us, let it make us handle the question of what really matters, what we really want. It raises the question of whether we have a target, whether we are overly preoccupied by things we have or things we have to do, whether we know the one thing that is of key importance to who we are and what we are about. It raises the question as to whether we are focused. The psalm's focus bears consideration. "One thing I ask of the LORD, this is what I seek: that I may dwell in the house of the LORD all the days of my life, to gaze upon the beauty of the LORD and to seek him in his temple" (v. 4).

Yahweh's house, Yahweh's beauty, Yahweh's temple sound like a fair focus. It is just the thing that John of the Cross wants us to focus on. When he pictures us deliberately imposing darkness on ourselves, he talks about us needing to be inclined:

> not to the easiest but to the most difficult, not to the most delightful but to the harshest, not to the most gratifying but to the less pleasant, not to what means rest but to hard work, not to the consoling but to the unconsoling. . . .
>
> To come to the pleasure you have not, you must go by a way you enjoy not; to come to the knowledge you have not, you must go by a way in which you know not; to come to the possession you have not, you must go by a way in which you possess not; to come to be what you are not, you must go by a way in which you are not.[2]

The statement is terribly negative, but it is meant to give us a focus, to strip us down, but to strip us down to what matters. It invites us to "one thing."

We are free not to volunteer for the self-imposed darkness, but if the other darkness comes to us, it imposes itself. It is a common feature of training for ministry. People give up the focus they had before and are on the way to another focus, but while they are training, they are in between. They may take to training like a duck to water, but they may hate it, and they may then lash out at the church and the seminary and the universities and—if they dare—God. When they do the last—lash out at God—then they are getting somewhere. They and God are doing serious business because they are in the dark and God put them there, and the question is what is God going to do about it. The answer is usually, "Nothing for a while," because quick salvation would short-circuit the process and rid them of the chance to discover who they are in this uncomfortable place with yesterday's focus taken away.

They are still free in relation to this darkness. They do not have to cooperate. God does not abandon them because they resist it. It will come to an end, and beginning a new ministry will give them a new focus, give them relief and a form of light, an escape from the darkness. But it will be a cheap escape, and the new focus will not be the psalm's focus. "One thing I ask of the Lord, this is what I seek." To serve God? To be ordained? "That I may dwell in the house of the Lord all the days of my life, to gaze upon the beauty of the Lord and to seek him in his temple." That is the "one thing" that is worth going for.

The psalm contains three facts about Yahweh. Yahweh has a house, Yahweh has beauty, and Yahweh has a temple. The fact that God has a house to live in reflects that Yahweh is a person. Admittedly, rather than having a proper, permanent, fixed, stone-built dwelling, Yahweh preferred a tent. This preference for camping is the aspect of the doctrine of God that I have always found most difficult to understand. But whether it was a tent or a house it meant that Yahweh was a person, and you could go up to this dwelling place and walk in and see Yahweh.

Yahweh has beauty. I have puzzled about that because it does not obviously fit with the rest of Psalm 27. This is not a soppy psalm. It is a gritty, robust, determined psalm, one that presupposes that Yahweh is a gritty, robust, determined kind of God. But the psalmist also believes in the grace, the goodness, and the attractiveness of Yahweh, and Yahweh's acts of grace and goodness also show that Yahweh is a gritty, robust, determined kind of God. Which fits with Yahweh having a palace, a rather splendid kind of house. Hebrew does not have a word for "temple" and uses the word used in other contexts for "palace," so that when "temple" occurs in the Old Testament, it is usually a word that reminds us that Yahweh is like a monarch with all the power and privilege of monarchy in the ancient world. Yahweh lives in a palace, but the door is open, and we can walk in and talk to the sovereign. "I have a personal, powerful God with all the attractiveness of that," says the psalm. "The one thing that I have asked, the one thing that I am seeking, is to live with that person, to ask that sovereign for things, to thrill at that robust and gritty God who is committed to me, who takes a 'one thing' attitude with me as if I were the only person in the world, because this God is able to do that with me and with each of my brothers and sisters."

And so I will walk through the darkness because there is light on the other side. Yahweh "will keep me safe in his dwelling; he will hide me in the shelter of his tabernacle and set me high upon a rock. Then my head will be exalted above the enemies who surround me; at his tabernacle will I sacrifice with shouts of joy; I will sing and make music to the LORD" (vv. 5–6).

The reference to Yahweh's tabernacle is noteworthy. The psalmist knows that Yahweh is still an incurable backpacker, even after the temple is built—always on the move, on to the next place, ahead of you or with you or following you, but never settling down. I will be there in God's dwelling, in God's company, eating and drinking and laughing with God. My ambition will be realized. There is that one thing I want, one thing I have focused on, and I am focusing on it the more because of the pressure of darkness. That is the nature of the experience if you let it have its way. It will produce the goods. The stripping down to one thing means focusing on that one thing and reaching it, because the one who drives you into darkness is really light and salvation.

When you are walking through the dark night, it is no use for someone else to tell you that it will come to an end. You have to say it to yourself, you have to be able to give assent to it for yourself. That is partly why John of the Cross wrote his books. He wanted you to read his account of how people came through the dark night and at least to know that you are not the first person to walk that way. That is what Psalm 27 wants. Knowing this does not mean that the darkness will stop being real darkness. But it does mean that you may be able to believe that darkness is not all there is, to imagine finding that "the LORD is my light and my salvation."

6

Friendship

During our mid-twenties, Ann and I experienced several major changes during a short period of time. Over a year or two or three, we ceased to be students, started work, got married, settled in an area where we had never lived before, and started a family. Whereas both of us had previously had a group of friends, mostly of our own sex, these five events worked together to produce a very different situation: We were not only each other's best friend but more or less each other's only friend. We could not keep up the old friendships in the same way, and events conspired against our making new friends. It did not seem to be a problem; indeed, I did not realize it was happening.

In a strange way, Ann's illness has changed all that. Over the period of years since Ann had to give up work, a number of people have reached into her life and become friends to her. It has been a mutual business; they are not merely people offering support to her and me. Over the more recent period since Ann's seizure, I have had the experience of a number of people elbowing their way into my life, as I think of it, more forcibly than people needed to do with Ann. It has made me aware of the friend-shaped hole that had been there for a while for both of us—because I doubt if God's design was for two people to be everything to each other. For me, they have been people who made me believe I was loved, people who asked questions that made me think new thoughts, and of course people who enabled me to stand when I might have fallen over.

So what is a friend? I suppose I am talking about someone you appreciate, someone you enjoy spending time with, someone you are especially glad to see, someone interesting. But of course there is more to it than that. A friend is someone you come to trust, someone you commit yourself to in some way. It is someone with whom you find yourself sharing who you are, sharing things you might not share with everyone. It is someone you want to do things for, give things to, when you know what they like.

In Hebrew and Greek, two of the common words for friend are related to words for love, and that tells you something about friendship. It is a form of love. And in Hebrew and Greek, love is a matter of mind, feelings, and action. You love God with mind and feelings and action, says Deuteronomy, because that is what love is like. Of course, our love is a reflection of God's. God loves with mind, feelings, and action. God appreciates us, enjoys spending time with us, is glad to see us, finds us interesting, trusts us, makes a commitment to us, shares intimate secrets with us.

And all that applies to human relationships. When you love a friend, this love, too, is a matter of mind, feelings, and action, like God's love for us and ours for God. And like love between us and God, it is two-way. A friendship would not work if only one of the two people wanted it.

God's friendship with us may be like our love for God in that it tends to develop gradually. We do not find that the whole of God is forced on us at once, and we do not give all of ourselves to God at once, even if there are moments when we take leaps forward in our awareness of being loved by God and of loving God. This, too, is true of human friendship. It comes about gradually as both parties subconsciously take the risk of letting it happen, stage by stage.

There is indeed risk. God takes risks in entrusting intimate secrets to us, in sharing the ministry of the Godhead in the world with us. We take risks with God in opening up our lives to heavenly scrutiny and looking at ourselves through God's eyes and saying we will do what God wants us to do and go where God wants us to go. We take risks in sharing our inner secrets with each other too, the risk of looking stupid and sinful and proud and narrow to the other person, and thus to ourselves.

Friendship takes time and energy too. That is why there are limits to the number of friends you can have, and why a married couple may find themselves making fewer friends than they did when they were single. God has infinite capacity to share with an infinite number of beings, with each of us. But we are not God, and we do not have the resources to share with everyone.

So what is the point of taking the risk and expending the energy? Why not hide from other people, as some people do? And why should friendship be the subject of Christian reflection? One reason is the way our friends change us. As in marriage, which is a form of friendship if you are lucky, our friends may decide they want to change us, and they may succeed in some ways, though these changes may be a bit external. (If you could see me, you might think that my clothes are garish. People said I would have an identity crisis in California because I would be just like everyone else, but even in California, people from the seminary president to the students make comments about my clothes, and my wife's neurologist even asked once if I was color-blind.)

The more profound changes come about when people are not trying. Some of them come about because we like something about a friend. It is one of the things we appreciate about them, and we find ourselves thinking the same way they do. They have changed us. Or maybe we think, "Well, if they believe that is important or interesting or worthwhile, perhaps there is something to it, or at least I would like to find out about it and understand it because it is part of them." Or we think, "That is off the wall. How can someone possibly think like that?" If it were anyone else, we would dismiss it, but because it is a friend, we do not dismiss it. We want to understand, because we love this other person. We may find that the thing that seemed off the wall is not so crazy after all when looked at through the prism of our friend's personality. We may end up changing our thinking and our attitudes and our lives and therefore our ministries. That is what friendship can do.

There is also a reverse process if you are friends. You yourself are off the wall in some ways. I know I am, because my colleagues have told me. (I looked up the expression in a dictionary, and it said "crazy." So I looked it up in a different dictionary, and it just said "unconventional," which I found more acceptable, so I bought that dictionary.) I find that a friend will ask me why I think or act a certain way, and I have to work it out and say it in a way I have not done so before. And by that process friends help you discover things about yourself.

Of course, the things you discover about yourself through your friendships may be things you do not like, and you may feel you want to change them. If you have fallen into really challenging friendships, your friends may not let you off the hook. One of the friendships I have most valued was like that. This friend would make the most outrageous, demanding observations about how I lived my life and how I ought to live it and how I thought about things and how I ought to think about them and how I saw myself and how I ought to see myself. I could not ignore these observations because they came out of love, and they risked changing me; indeed, they did change me. In a way, this chapter and maybe every chapter in this book is the fruit of friendship. Your friends change you, and therefore, they change your ministries.

That is the upside of friendship. There are two aspects of the downside that occur to me. I have already hinted at one. There can be a sadness about making friends in some circumstances because they are likely to have a limited life. Most friendships, even the deep ones, have a short sell-by date. The single toughest aspect of our move from Britain to America was having to cut ties with friends and family.

It is our own experience of something people at seminary go through each year. On the last day of the seminary year in June, we distribute the "Ember List," a leaflet containing the photographs of those leaving and details of where they are going so that people can pray for them. It includes some biographical data that people write themselves. One of the things people often comment on is the importance of the friendships they made at the seminary, the people they got to know. That same day is also the day when everyone is saying good-bye, and a few tears are shed. So the last day of the year brings out the upside and the downside of the fact that the friendships people make are among the most important things of their time at seminary.

One person said to me one year in some anguish, "Why does God always take people away?" She was moving to a parish in a part of the country where she had never lived before and was having once more to start again. She had had to leave the people she loved in her hometown to go to the place where she had spent most of her working life before seminary, then she had had to leave the people she loved there to come to seminary, now she had to leave the people she loved in seminary. You may be able to keep up one or two friendships by occasional visits, and you can talk to people on the phone, but many of the friendships cannot continue to grow in the way they could before.

A few weeks after commencement one year, Ann and I had lunch with a couple we had gotten to know and who had left. It was lovely to be able to do that, but I found myself feeling sad even while I was there. I realized that this reunion was reminding me that we would hardly ever see this couple again. Such meetings are more like reminders of something that once was rather than a growing development of something.

Our friends become part of us and we of them. One reason for this is the process of mutual influence I have described. As Ann and I have been in the midst of saying good-byes, I have found myself often singing the line from a Paul Young song: "Every time you go away you take a little part of me." In the song, the phrase applies to romantic love; it seems to me to apply to friendship. The same is true of Ella Fitzgerald's classic "Every Time We Say Good-bye, I Die a Little."

There is another aspect to the poignancy of all this. When you get to know someone, one of the paradoxical results is that you realize there is so much more to know. I suppose the converse must be true. The more you let yourself be known, the more there is that you might learn about yourself and the more you might be able to grow if the friendship continues.

In John 15, Jesus talks about God pruning us, and I can only think that separating from friends, losing them in this sense, is part of the pruning process that is involved in life. The loss of friends, therefore, can help us grow. Things are taken away not because there is no growth and not to prevent growth but to encourage growth. Outside their kitchen window, friends of ours had some tomato plants that they had inherited from their cottage's previous occupant. The plants had lovely yellow flowers and some little green tomatoes. Our friends did not know that to grow proper tomatoes in England, you have to stop the pretty yellow flowers from growing past the fourth branch. When God takes away or when life takes away or when the system takes away, God can use the situation to produce fruit. This positive effect does not take away the sadness involved, but it may take the edge off the sadness. The cost may be worth what we give each other and what we gain.

There is another downside involved in making friends, a risk that headlines in newspapers periodically make us aware of, the risk that friendship love can turn into romantic love. I do not know any surefire way of ensuring that this does not happen. Now, for people who are in a position to fall in love, that may be fine, and no doubt falling in love with a friend is a better idea than trying to make friends with someone you have fallen in love with. There are guidelines for pastoral relationships that can help one avoid the particular forms of risk in those relationships, but the same issues arise in friendships.

When Harry Met Sally is my all-time number 3 favorite film (behind Paris, Texas and Once upon a Time in America, with Leaving Las Vegas recently reaching number 4). On a good day, what I now feel about When Harry Met Sally is the same as what I feel about that Stanley Hauerwas remark in chapter 4: Its thesis is deeply illuminating but actually wrong. The movie's theme is that men and women can never be friends because sex will always get in the way. Even if it does not for the woman, it will for the man, and that is enough.

We live in a generation in which many marriages fall apart and in which many people have affairs, and that is true of Christians and it is true of clergy. In any congregation or among any group of clergy, there will thus be a significant number who will have affairs one day and a significant number whose marriages will break down. I do not believe it is possible to predict who it will be nor for any of us to be sure "it will not be me."

I have had several experiences of women telling me they have fallen in love with me when I had no such feelings for them. I have also had the experience of getting sexually entangled with someone and thus doing wrong by her, by Ann, by God—and by the people who think I am an upright man who does a good job of living with the loss involved in his wife's illness. I recently received a letter from a student who said this:

> In the past few years I have witnessed marriages fall apart and heard of affairs that seemed to unsuspectedly creep up on the most godly of couples, and years and years of marriage end in divorce, regret, and bitterness. Last year I myself ended a relationship with my "steady" of two years partly because I had grown so cynical about marriage and about what love was. But just sitting with you two and talking and hearing you share your lives with me was really refreshing. . . . I thanked God for that glimmer of hope, for showing me that marriage can work and that love can endure the most difficult circumstances.

I wish the student's letter were more unequivocally justified. Harry's thesis is one I myself have had to take more seriously. Yet I do not think it is necessarily a universal truth. If it is indeed difficult to predict who might have an affair, that is a frightening fact, but it may be even more likely to affect us if we do not acknowledge it. Having true, deep friendships may make having an affair more likely, but such friendships may have the opposite effect, because such friendships are a resource to us. Perhaps each of us needs to come to an understanding of our own degree of security or weakness in this connection and to an assessment of how far we can with safety encourage such friendships. With hindsight, I can see that I ought to have been able to see my own insecurity, but I did not. I have had to try to let God put the situation right afterward.

By its nature, ministry with other people is dangerous, because it involves relationship, and relationships are dangerous. I guess it has always been so, though it is tempting to believe that there are ways in which the dangers are especially marked in our culture. One danger about such relationships is the possibility of using people and abusing them, of making them the victims of our desires for power and control. Perhaps sex is just another such danger zone.

But there are things we can do to reduce the risk. We can minister in threes rather than one-on-one. We can talk with someone such as a spiritual director about our friendships. We can look for the signs that suggest romantic love rather than friendship and be prepared to act on what we find. I suspect that is the biggest thing, for our culture assumes that if it is love, it must be right, and we are subject to the temptation to think the same thing.

For some of us, of whom I am one, this is an area in which we will have to accept pruning. Such pruning on God's part can carve space in our lives, take us away from our idols, remove us to a foreign country, enlarge our understanding of God, and enable us to discover who we are.

Although I did once grow tomatoes, I know virtually nothing else about gardening, but I did once discover something about vines. We were driving through the Vale of Hebron in the West Bank, where some of the best vines grow. It was the first time I had visited the country in the spring, and I had never seen vines in their pruned state. They were a terrible sight. Six months before this they would have been flourishing plants that had grown so extravagantly that they would have curled like a bower over your head so that you could have reached up and let the fresh grapes fall into your mouth. But they had been cut down so that they were nothing more than black gnarled stumps a foot or two high. We cannot have grapes without being willing to be a vine. We cannot be a vine without being willing to be pruned. We cannot grow grapes next year without being pruned. But we can grow grapes this year, and our friends can help us.

7

Hope

Not the End of the Story

Imagine that a tourism tycoon announces a competition for the designing of a new hotel in Sarajevo or Belfast or Freetown or whatever city happens to be off-limits as a vacation destination when you read this. Imagine that she gives the award to a wondrous plan for an eight-story complex with restaurants, jacuzzis, saunas, discos, and swimming pools. Not only so, but she sends the plans out to tender and gives the contract to a construction company.

One day in the 580s B.C., Jeremiah the prophet contracted to buy some land in circumstances that were about as absurd (see Jeremiah 32). For the second time in a decade, Judah is under invasion from the Babylonians as punishment for wanting to run its own life, and Jerusalem is under siege. Jeremiah himself is in prison in Jerusalem. He had been going about declaring that the city would again fall to the Babylonians and that the best thing to do was surrender. This understandably displeased the political authorities, who viewed Jeremiah as a collaborator, a traitor, and a danger to community morale.

Things are evidently little better for Jeremiah's family. Their village of Anathoth lies a few miles north of Jerusalem, across the crucial line that divides northern Israel from southern Judah. Where Jeremiah came from was no doubt another reason for the Jerusalem authorities' deep suspicion of him. He was, after all, not actually one of them.

One can guess that having the Babylonian army camped on your doorstep as it besieges Jerusalem does nothing for the quality of life in Anathoth. Perhaps this is why Jeremiah's cousin Hanamel asks Jeremiah if he wants to buy a piece of land from him. When things are bad, people often have to turn their assets into cash. That might mean selling your animals; in due course, it might mean selling yourself and/or members of your family into slavery for a while. In between, it might mean selling some or all of your land (technically, leasing it). But you could not sell your land to just anyone. The land had been allocated by God to the tribes and families of Israel, and it had to stay in the family. You had to see if any of your relatives could and would buy it. So Hanamel pays a prison visit to Jeremiah, not out of concern for the prisoner's welfare but out of concern for his own.

Whether we think of the city of Jerusalem, the people of Judah and Israel, or the personal circumstances of Jeremiah or Hanamel, we find reason for gloom or anxiety at best, despair and hopelessness at worst. It may resonate with the gloom, anxiety, despair, and hopelessness that we all know. In many traditional denominations, there is reason enough for such gloom as they contemplate reduced congregations and economic difficulties. In individual churches, outward flourishing can sometimes conceal deep division or persistent inward-lookingness that has become the despair of their leaders. The jobs of individual Christians may cause them deep anxieties, whether they work in schools or in business or in industry—or if they have no job at all. In the dark hours of the night, people can experience hopelessness as they ask themselves whether their marriages are in terminal decline or how on earth they can handle or help their children.

In a context of gloom, anxiety, hopelessness, and despair, at community and individual levels, Jeremiah puts his shekels on the table and buys the piece of land from Hanamel. I wonder whether Hanamel could hardly believe his luck, whether he danced back to Anathoth laughing at the foolishness of the unworldly-wise prophet in buying land at this perilous moment in history. Is Jeremiah one tribe short of a chosen people, one candle short of a menorah? Why did he do it?

He did it because God told him to. Sometimes we have the experience of knowing that God is pointing us in a direction that seems risky or stupid and is looking to see how we respond. At the same time denominations are having a hard time finding jobs for their clergy, people are still resigning jobs they like because they believe God is calling them to pastoral ministry. Humanly speaking, they seem to be making unwise decisions.

After buying the land, Jeremiah learns more. It is often the case that only after something happens do we see why God looked for a particular step or allowed a particular thing to happen. In Jeremiah's case, buying the land was a sign that the invasion of the country and the siege of the city by the Babylonians were not the end of the story. One day fields and vineyards would again be worth selling here. God had not finished with the city of Jerusalem, with the people of Judah and Benjamin, and with individual people such as Jeremiah and Hanamel. God still had their destiny in mind.

After signing the contract, Jeremiah offers God a prayer that seems to read more like a history lesson. He summarizes how God created the world, delivered Israel from Egypt, gave them their land, and how this story now seems to be coming to an end in Babylonian occupation. There is some irony in the fact that Jeremiah himself does not seem to see the point of his own story. As is often the case, his question contains the seed of its own answer. How can God let this story come to an end? Of course, God cannot. The promise of the prophets of the exile is that the promises of God that go back to Abraham still apply. They just need restating. Arguably, that is all these prophets do. The hope of Jerusalem, Judah, Benjamin, Jeremiah, and Hanamel is the hope of a story and a divine commitment that go back to Abraham.

The hope of the church and of individual Christians lies in the same realities, the same story, and the same commitment, now underlined by what God has done in Jesus. Might the church die out? Denominations may die out—old denominations, and new ones that now seem vibrant and full of life. Patterns of ministry may change. Congregations may grow and shrink. Jobs may change. Marriages may break down, parents may make terrible mistakes, and children may turn their backs on them. All these things may indeed happen before our eyes. But they have written over them the promise that "houses, fields, and vineyards will again be bought in this land" (see Jer. 32:42–44). As the church we are entitled to be certain that God is committed to us, for the church itself is the fruit of the original unbreakable commitment to Abraham. As individuals we are entitled to the certainty that God is working out a purpose for us, that the promise embraces us.

Yes, says God, this city is to be given into the hands of the Babylonians. And when that happens, it will be nasty. The king, for instance, will be blinded as an act of sadistic punishment, before he is taken off to Babylon, and as another act of sadistic punishment the last sight his eyes will see, the last image Zedekiah will take with him to Babylon, is the sight of his two sons being killed. But all this will not be the end. After that, "I will surely gather them from all the lands where I banish them. . . . I will bring them back to this place and will let them live in safety. They will be my people, and I will be their God. . . . I will rejoice in doing them good and will assuredly plant them in this land with all my heart and soul" (Jer. 32:37–38, 41).

It's not over till it's over. The moments of justified anxiety, gloom, hopelessness, and despair stand under the promise of God. We may not be able to see how God can bring fruitfulness from them until afterward, but we can believe that God will.

Soaking and Hoping

Hoping is a familiar biblical and theological theme. Soaking is one I invented.

I once took part in a Holy Week retreat. It involved going to more church services than any other week of my life and reading the gospel story in every possible version, the sections of the epistles that expound on the significance of Jesus' passion, and most of the psalms that were on Jesus' lips during the last days of his life. Toward the end of that week I felt as if I had been enveloped, soaked, immersed in the passion story in a powerful way. No matter what else I did that week, I could not get away from the passion story.

We inevitably live our lives in the world and in the church not by the passion story but by the values and the story of the world and of our own experience. What we mostly need in our Christian lives is not a new truth that no one has told us yet but the old truth coming home to us afresh month by month and year by year. This truth will then shape our thinking and our lives. We need to be immersed in that counter-story, the one that opposes the world's story.

It so happened that after celebrating the resurrection at the dawning of Easter Sunday, I then flew to Israel. On the Monday following Easter I was sitting in my favorite place in all the world, the terrace of the YMCA guest house, Peniel-by-Galilee, looking out over the Sea of Galilee. I began to do something I had often told students to do but had never done myself—read through the Galilee half of Mark's Gospel while sitting in a place where I could actually see Capernaum, Bethsaida, Chorazim, and other places traditionally associated with events in Jesus' life. I soaked myself in the pre-passion story, visualizing it unfolding before my eyes. But it was also Easter Week, and I continued working through the day-by-day lectionary readings, many of which focus on Galilee: "Get up to Galilee," Jesus says as soon as he is risen, and near the Sea of Galilee Jesus asks Peter questions about love and commissions him. At the same time the lectionary had us reading through 1 Peter; its beginning asserts that Jesus' resurrection rebirths us to a living hope.

For me that was the link between soaking and hoping. Soaking in the reality of the story of Jesus as the one who lived and taught and ministered and died and rose for me reminded me of the basis for living hope. The soaking was key to the hoping. If I was to be a person of hope, it was on the basis of that story and being soaked in it.

This experience happened at a time when I needed it. I had been going through a frustrating period of my life, not succeeding in completing a project I wanted to finish, and I had become clinically depressed. As it happened I had attended some lectures on pastoral theology, lectures on "Hoping and Wishing." The lecturer referred quite often to hopelessness, and I realized that each time he said the word it hurt me deep down. I realized that my depression and hopelessness were related. One can become depressed or hopeless about particular things from time to time, but they can trip you into general hopelessness; that was what had happened to me.

But I also realized that you can become aware of the reality of hopelessness, the reasons for it, only when you have realized that there are reasons for hope. It is unwise to think about hoping until you know there is a basis for it. It is difficult to face up to hopelessness until you know there might be an answer to it, a way of facing it.

I once said to Ann, "Would you like a pastry with your cup of tea?" She replied, "Have you got one?" She was wise. She did not wish to be conned into playing with the idea of a pastry if I was about to reply, "Tough. I forgot to buy some." First discover if there is something to hope for, then hope for it.

The good news of the gospel is that the God and Father of our Lord Jesus Christ has given us a new birth to a living hope through the resurrection of Jesus Christ from the dead. We hide from our hopelessness. But there are grounds for hope, and therefore, it can be faced.

Isaiah 25 promises a day when the veil of mourning will be taken away from everyone and God will wipe away the tears from everyone's eyes. God promises to handle our individual pains and griefs and the reproach of the people of God that is also so depressing.

We are invited to name our hopelessness, in our lives, the church, and the world, because the resurrection of Jesus makes it possible to risk doing that. His resurrection is the guarantee that there is hope in all these areas. That does not resolve the dialectic between glory and pain. Indeed, in facing hopelessness, we are taken back into the pain of the cross. But doing so does not leave us with nothing, with unacknowledged pain.

We are invited to name our hopelessness and to let ourselves be soaked, enfolded, immersed in the counter-story of Jesus' life, death, and resurrection, because they are the basis for hope.

L'Arche

Just north of Paris at Trosly-Breuil is the original home of the l'Arche community, which brings together disabled and nondisabled people to share their lives. One weekend Ann and I were there for a gathering of twenty professors, bishops, and others from France, Belgium, Canada, and Britain to discuss the theology of disability—or rather, as the invitation put it, "to discuss how Jesus touches us in and through the poor, the broken, and the weak"—in the light of our own experience. The program consisted chiefly of simply sharing our testimonies.

I have referred already to the ministry Ann exercises within the seminary and elsewhere. When I go off to speak at a conference, often the thing people take away is not anything I said but their meeting with Ann, though they rarely articulate what affected them. My guess is that she embodies human characteristics that belong to us all but that we normally seek to evade, such as fragility, dependence, and uncertainty. She brings these demons out into the open in such a way that they cease to be demons. Indeed, she reveals that they are angels. They are part of being human, part of the nakedness that humanity originally wore without shame, and they are therefore part of imaging God. Disabled people in their fragility, dependence, and uncertainty embody the other side of that image. Ann affirms the presence of God with her in her disability.

Disability through an illness such as multiple sclerosis is not the same as the usually lifelong disability of the handicapped members of l'Arche, but it raises overlapping human and theological questions, as well as some questions of its own. The woman I married was not fragile, dependent, and uncertain but a person of independence, initiative, drive, and energy who kept many balls in the air and in some respects behaved like a feminist before such was invented. I have been married to two personalities within the same body yet to one human being. This must relativize the importance of personality in the sense that the notion is so important to us and must point to a less self-contained basis for understanding the intrinsically human.

One consistent feature of Ann is the web of relationships in which she has been involved with family and friends. As the original Genesis 1 statement about the creation of humanity implies, being human is being in relationship with other people—including the disabled. Our essential humanity and value lie in being in relationships of receiving and giving. This is true for disabled and nondisabled alike, but the former may unveil the fact.

Another feature of Ann is the continuous story she has lived. The story bridges the change in who she is, and it is destined to continue toward those transforming changes that will embrace us all. It must be, then, that such changes do not threaten what authentic humanity means. Everyone has a story, even the most disabled, the most poor, the most unpleasant, and the most wicked, and it is often their stories that are the most worth hearing and the most illuminating.

Another consistent feature of Ann is her physical body, recognizably one even with all the changes that have come about because of those wretchedly sclerosed myelin sheathes that prevent messages from passing between brain and limbs. The physical continuity in who Ann is draws attention to the important physical base to human personality. The entire life of l'Arche depends on the assumption that our bodies really matter to us as human beings. That may seem self-evident, but Christian faith has often been dualistic, reckoning that the body is a mere dispensable shell around the real person. That conflicts with the fact that God created our bodies and intends to transform them. People who cannot speak make especially clear how essential the body is to communication.

Part of the philosophy of l'Arche is that the relationship between the disabled and the nondisabled is two-way. Each gains from the other. People who work in l'Arche communities speak movingly of the ministry the disabled exercise. "Every person, even the most handicapped, is called to be a source of grace and of peace for the whole community, for the Church and for humanity," declares a flyer for the related Faith and Light movement, which brings together families with disabled people for sharing, fiesta, celebration, and prayer. And when it comes to celebration, says the Faith and Light charter, the handicapped are often less disabled than others because they are not imprisoned by convention, worried about efficiency, or fearful of what others may think. They live more simply in the present moment, their humility and transparency making them naturally disposed toward community festivity.

It is possible for the disabled to be the victims of other people's needs to organize, dominate, or do miracles. God does not organize, dominate, or do miracles for Ann. God lets her be. Perhaps she ministers to God. I know personally that the disabled exercise an important ministry to the nondisabled. As I suggested in the introduction, I would be a different person were it not for the positive shaping effect Ann's disability has had on me. I know she slows me down, for good; often we would be processing through the seminary dining room with half the seminary behind us, but I had the impression no one complained. She makes me appreciate simple things, like squirrels and clouds and the swaying of the willow tree outside our house in Nottingham. It is my own confirmation of an insight that underlies the l'Arche philosophy that we gain from sharing a mode of existence that is contemplative rather than activistic. This is an important witness regarding the nature of theology, church, and world.

There is another shaping too. One of my best friends once called me volatile, unpredictable in how I react depending on how I am inside. Ann's illness frees both tears and frustration, both love and anger, both resilience and guilty powerlessness ("Why can't I make it okay?"). Giving yourself to the poor or disabled, someone at l'Arche commented, can be the equivalent of going into the solitude of the desert to be confronted by the demons within.

It is often difficult to convince Ann of the positive effect she has on other people and on me. Indeed, I myself am not sure exactly what the nature of that effect is, as I do not know who I would be if I were not Ann's husband, shaped by who she is. We and God use her, without scruple (as Paul has God affirming, "I will have mercy on whom I have mercy, and I will have compassion on whom I have compassion" [Rom. 9:15]). We and God gain from her disability. For her there is often no felt gain. It is wholly loss. I trust that God grieves over that.

Someone during the weekend said, "The handicapped person helps us discover our own identity. Our gifts and competence are never adequate, and they transform these in order that we may respond to their real needs; we thereby discover who we are. In addition, they discover who they are by what they call forth in us." I dearly wish all this to be true, and I believe it is true up to the last sentence. Ann now has less comprehension of who she is than she had ten years ago and little comprehension of what she calls forth in people. We must no more romanticize the disabled than marginalize them.

Over tea on the Sunday afternoon of that weekend, I made a point of having a conversation with Frances Young, one of its organizers, whose severely disabled son is the subject of her book *Face to Face*. I wanted to say how much I had appreciated the opportunity to talk about Ann and me in the presence of people who knew from their own experience what I meant. She gave me an awesomely fierce hug and said something like, "I hope there will be something positive for you in the end." They were almost the last words that were said to me before we left, and they were going around in my head and my heart for the next thirty-six hours. They somehow brought to the surface a hopelessness that I feel about Ann and that I had not quite confessed to myself but had apparently communicated in my testimony. Now I feel like John Cleese (in a wonderful moment in the film *Clockwise*, I think), when he says, "It's not the despair I can't stand; it's the hope." (Actually, I subsequently discovered that what Frances said to me over tea was that she hoped I had gained something positive out of the weekend; I think Freud commented on how significant our mishearings are.)

I refer to hopelessness in this age, of course. The fact that Ann will be raised in Jesus to dance in the New Jerusalem is important to both of us. I once used to say to students that I would not mind if Rudolf Bultmann were right that this life is all we have, but I no longer say that.

Yet I must not give the wrong impression even about this age. One day as I stood in my office, looking out over the courtyard, I cried out to God, "I can't do it," and God replied, "You'll just have to." That sounds hard, but in a strange way it came as reassurance. It reminds me now of Gerhard von Rad's emphasis on the revelation of the Torah to Israel being a gift rather than an imposition. If God lays an expectation on you, it will not be one impossible to fulfill. Since then I have often cried out, "Will it be all right?" and have always known God to say yes. And it always has been.

Born to Run?

In his comments on Bruce Springsteen in *Hungry for Heaven*, Steve Turner suggests that a tension between humanity's "heavenly calling" and "earthly imprisonment" is the theme of Springsteen's best work. "In a typical small-town situation he sees two different sorts of people. There are those who resign themselves to mediocrity and those who burn with a passion to transcend their circumstances."[1]

In my last St. John's gig, I sang "Born to Run" to student bemusement. With wonderful melodrama it relates the way someone whose life feels hopeless urges Wendy to get out of this empty town with him, to let him in to be her friend and guard her "dreams and visions," to join him in going somewhere where they can walk in the sun. "But till then tramps like us, baby, we were born to run."

But "having articulated a religious question, [Springsteen] doesn't have a religious answer. Springsteen, I believe, realizes that a religious answer is needed and compensates by dressing essentially existential advice in glorious heavenly language."[2] In contrast, Christians have the religious answer but often don't articulate the question.

8

Identity

I have talked about the release we experience when we put down a burden and let our tensed muscles relax and the way it may be only then that we realize we were carrying a heavy load. The experience of doing this can also raise questions of identity, for carrying responsibilities is integral to identity for many of us.

A few years ago Ann and I had our first vacation together on our own after our two sons had grown up, and somehow it brought home to me a frightening realization about who I was—namely, Ann's husband. At center I was not a theologian or a teacher or a minister or a scholar or a principal—those were not what defined who I was. I was the husband of this disabled person. That was what shaped my life and my being as nothing else did, which meant, I realized (and this was the frightening bit), that when Ann died, I would not know who I was. This did not imply that I had reason to think she might die soon; indeed, she might outlive me. People with multiple sclerosis have a shorter life expectancy than other people, but men have a shorter life expectancy than women, so those two considerations cancel each other out. The point was that thinking about Ann's eventual death raised this question for me.

I realized that threatening fact anew when she had her seizure. When she was admitted to the hospital, a neurologist reassured me that she would fully recover, but as she lay in a bed unable to move, except for the one arm that flapped about with a mind of its own, this was not easy to believe. The nursing staff did not believe it either. ("I don't think she will ever feed herself again," one said.) For that matter, the neurologist later told me that he was not sure he had believed his own words, but I guess he was going by the book, and he was right. Indeed, some weeks after leaving the hospital Ann actually had more mobility than she had before her seizure. Someone told me of a woman in the United States who was cured of multiple sclerosis through being struck by lightning (I have not sought out thunderstorms to see if we can repeat the trick); perhaps Ann's seizure had a little of the same effect.

But in those dark early morning hours when I did not know what was happening, I wondered if she were dying. In those early days in the hospital, I again found myself thinking the selfish thought that if she died I would not know who I was, because my identity (I felt) was defined by her. Who would I be if I did not have this responsibility? If I think of "me" apart from Ann, what do I mean by the notion of "me"? If I answered, "Who I might be is a good-looking man with a full head of brown hair," it might make the idea of not having the burden attractive. But it makes me feel insecure.

Many years ago, before we knew that Ann might one day be wheelchair-bound, we knew a man whose wife had a chronic illness and was in a wheelchair. He always looked disheveled and unshaven, but I thought that was just the way he was. Then we lost touch with them, and his wife died. After a year or two, he remarried. Shortly after that we met him again, and he had been transformed into someone who looked smart and bright and alive. I wonder whether there is some sense in which I am at the former stage. I know that Ann is a different person from the one she once was, and so am I.

Because Ann was in the hospital after her seizure I had to go to the seminary midweek dinner on my own. Instead of walking in with her on my arm, I walked in alone. I felt like a stranger in a strange place. Without Ann I did not know who I was. Any husband or wife feels that way to a degree, but it seems especially true of me because I am the husband of someone with a grim illness and because the handling of that is so central in the shaping of my life. Are we only a series of potentials that become realized, but only in part, in relation to the people we become involved with and the experiences that happen to us? If so, I could have been realized in some other way. And the potentials are still there—I could still be realized in other ways.

Oddly, however, living virtually without Ann for those four weeks and living and relating to other people in new ways also strangely reassured me that there is a person here who exists in his own right, a person who one day I might get to know but who perhaps for the moment is suppressed.

I was thinking about all this when one day I heard the Jimmy Ciff song "Many Rivers to Cross." Out of interest, and perhaps with a view to singing it one day, I settled down to work out all the words. I soon found myself in tears over them because they expressed so much of what I was feeling about life at that time. There are many rivers to cross and "it's only my will that keeps me alive." Maybe "I merely survive because of my pride." And the loneliness won't leave me alone because the person I once knew is gone, and all sorts of temptations assail me, but I just have to keep looking for a way to cross rivers.

I think there is a link between this and a picture that has developed in my mind. I see myself pushing Ann's wheelchair toward the horizon. I am viewing us from behind, so I see my back and a bit of the wheelchair—I cannot see Ann. It is a bare landscape, and there is quite a distance to the horizon toward which I push, but the ground is fairly level and the pushing just requires commitment, grit, and persistence. A key point is that the distance to the horizon is finite and I cannot see how far the journey goes beyond the horizon. In theory, there may be many horizons to travel (many rivers to cross), but I do not have to visualize or face the fact of that long journey—just the one horizon. Perhaps that may be the only one, so that the pushing ends just beyond it. The other key point is that the two of us are alone, and thus I am the only one pushing. A single horizon and a lone pusher— on my own by my willpower I can manage just one horizon at a time.

The alternative picture that started to nudge into my thinking has two elements to it. First, I see the picture from above, as happens in a film when the camera is elevated on a camera crane. The horizon lengthens vastly, and I can see that the journey, the push, is much, much longer than I can see from ground level. There are indeed many rivers. There is no longer any way to avoid the prospect of the push lasting ten or twenty years, not just two or five.

The other element is that I see other people, in ones and twos and threes, coming to join me behind the wheelchair. Some are people I know; some are people I do not yet know; some are people I have known. Some just walk with me. Some take a handle. Some gently nudge me out of the way and push the wheelchair themselves. Ann is content as long as someone is pushing. I walk with them in the little crowd, content, more relaxed, unaccustomed to the luxury of walking without pushing. We talk quite a bit and laugh quite a bit. Someone ruffles my hair. The people change—some walk alongside longer than others. The number of them changes—sometimes there are one or two, sometimes eight or ten. From where I am, because of the other people, I can no longer see whether the countryside is bare, nor am I so aware of the distance to the horizon or how far we have traveled. I can now commit myself to the ten or twenty years while still living in the present, rather than being tempted to postpone living until some future that may never come.

One of the results of Ann's seizure was indeed that some people forced their way into my life out of love for me and for her. That forcing continued after the crisis was over. It might have been tempting to assume that people were sorry for us and/or were being "pastoral," and if that had been so, I would still have appreciated it. But it became clear that these people were not merely feeling sorry for me or being pastoral; they were helping because they liked me.

I feel self-conscious writing that last phrase, which is significant because I do not often feel self-conscious. Over a period of a year or two, however, I got used to the idea that some people enjoy my company.

What is it that makes me, or anyone else, attractive to someone? Again, there are paradoxes here. If we are describing a friend to someone, we probably refer to some attributes. By implication, I enjoy that person's company because he is sensitive or fun or because he likes rock 'n' roll or is an interesting theologian. Yet it is not actually a specifiable list of attributes that draws us into friendship with people. It is more like an intuitive sense that there is someone attractive here. Perhaps everyone is likeable in this sense—the question is whether that likeableness is on the surface and is recognized or hidden.

There is then an important dialectical relationship between knowing and loving. Having begun to know, I begin to love. Beginning thus to love, I get to know more because the other person is more willing to be known. Getting to know more, I love more because I understand more. Loving more, I get to know more. And that goes on forever. This is true of relationships among human beings and between us and God.

If the knowing is not merely having a list of attributes, what is it? To judge from the way the Bible works, knowing involves narrative. The knowing comes about through listening to stories. When we want to characterize each other, we will often do so by telling a story that sums up the person.

In the Bible, God is known as one who has certain attributes. The classic list comes first in Exodus 34 and often recurs: Yahweh is compassionate and gracious, long-tempered and abounding in love and faithfulness, though in the end not soft. But that characterization of God comes in the midst of a narrative that extends from Genesis to Kings and shows up in Chronicles, Ezra, Nehemiah, Esther, Ruth, Jonah, and elsewhere. Those narratives do all sorts of things, but one thing they do is establish who God is. Stories do that. They give life to adjectives and nouns.

After a number of sessions with the counselor to whom I referred in chapter 5, eventually he and I began to wonder whether we had done the main business, whether we were to go anywhere else from here or simply call it a day. About that time we had a time of prayer for healing in a seminary chapel service, and I felt compelled to go for prayer. The person who prayed with me said she felt I had a barrier around me preventing access. She wondered whether the shield was there not to keep other people out but to keep me out. God was inviting me to discover who I was, to let myself into myself. It was immediately clear what the counseling agenda needed to be. God was bidding me discover who I was.

A day or two later, I had to compose a paragraph about myself for some purpose. Such paragraphs usually go, "The Rev. Dr. John Goldingay is principal of St. John's College, Nottingham. He has written a number of books on the Old Testament. He is married to Ann, who has multiple sclerosis." As I have hinted, I have been tempted to think that in real terms all it need say is the last sentence. That is who I am. I decided to try to say who I was irrespective of work and began, "John Goldingay is an enthusiast about rock, blues, and jazz."

I told all this to the counselor. When I got to the last bit, he shot bolt upright in his chair. "Yes! You're an enthusiast." In my mind, the stress had been on what I was enthusiastic about, but he showed me another, more important implication of what I had written. There was something about my personality in the word *enthusiast,* and I could immediately recognize it, though I had not seen it as clearly before.

This is an example both of the usefulness of adjectives and nouns and also of loving and thus knowing. The counselor's uncharacteristic outburst was an expression of love, the more powerful because of its rarity, that had provided both insight into him and into me. I remember feeling that there was an empty outline of the shape of a person before me, like a child's drawing, and that I now had the first word, the first attribute, to put inside it.

For a while I had a hard time finding other words to put into the person-shaped figure. I can think of two reasons for that. One is that some words, like *vulnerability,* are related to Ann, and I wanted to find things that were not contingent on that relationship. The other is that I did not quite dare to believe the words, even when they came from other people. I guess this is one reason why I am going to list only five: imaginative, colorful, physical, unassuming, dangerous.

Because of something one of our students happened to say over lunch, I told him about the visit to the counselor and about discovering I was an enthusiast. The college is named after St. John the Evangelist, and the student later told me he had been thinking about St. John the Enthusiast as an equivalent to St. John the Evangelist. That made me remember that *enthusiast* comes from a Greek word that means "filled with God" or "inspired." My enthusiasm could be something from God and through which God worked. The same is true of being imaginative and creative, because God is the very source of imagination and creativity. Discovering things about identity is actually related to living for God.

One example: I used to get angry with Ann when I felt she slighted me—when she seemed to talk to me as if I were incredibly stupid for misunderstanding her. Once, we were on a journey. "Where are we?" she asked as we left a restaurant. "Near Weston-super-Mare," I replied. "I mean where is the car," she retorted. I then snapped at her for talking to me that way, and I told her never to do it again. She got angry and cried. Before we went to bed we made up, but I knew it was an example of something that happens from time to time. Her frustration with her lot finds expression in hostility to me, and for some reason I find it difficult to cope with that particular expression of it. Eventually, I realized it was because it brings back memories from childhood (not that my mother ever intended to be scathing, any more than Ann does). Now that I have realized that this is what happens, I am less vulnerable to it. Discovering things about identity could even be something that relates to living with other people.

_____ 9

Joy

"He will be a joy and delight to you, and many will rejoice because of his birth," the angel said to Zechariah (Luke 1:14). And when Elizabeth saw Mary, the baby in Elizabeth's womb "leaped for joy" (1:44). When John was born, neighbors and relatives "shared her joy" (1:58). And when the angels appeared to the shepherds, they brought them news of "great joy" for everyone (2:10).

What is joy? First, let us not be rude about noisiness. The kind of rejoicing the Bible talks most about is a noisy affair. It is a matter of celebration, loud music, shouting, dancing. When there is joy about, it can be heard a long way off. Joy is associated with harvest and winning battles, with feasting and drinking. Thus, when the Bible talks about relationships with God, it assumes they are noisy affairs. Modern books on spirituality tend to imply that spirituality is an "introvert" business. They talk about going to the depths and about the journey inward and so on. Most of the time the Bible's spirituality of joy is an "extrovert" spirituality. It is a spirituality for the majority, an asset in mission and ministry, and also an invitation to people such as scholars and writers to let their less dominant side find expression.

But many Christians are introverts and maybe need to start somewhere else. In odd corners of the Bible, introverts can find a joy for themselves. Psalm 4:7 says, "You have filled my heart with greater joy than when their grain and new wine abound." Jeremiah, that great introvert, wrote, "Your words . . . were my joy and my heart's delight" (15:16). I suppose it is a sign of the dominance of introvert spirituality that we think of joy as a matter of the heart. It is closely related to peace, I think. Peace is an inner acceptance of things, but it is more passive than joy. Joy is an inner liftedness of spirit that means we do more than just cope inside when things are tough; we are happy inside even if things are difficult outside.

One summer someone said to me, "You're not bad at producing the fruit of the Spirit really, except joy. You're not very good at joy." It made me think, of course. I knew that I was often morose, for personality and circumstantial reasons, and not very good at hiding my feelings. So I asked God for a spirit of joy, and God gave me that, for much of the latter part of that summer. Humanly speaking, joy had been possible because it was summer and I had shed some of my responsibilities. When I had to take on responsibilities again, joy went. So I asked God to give it back, not expecting that to work, and God did. Then it went again under pressure, but I knew that was the case in part because of neglect. But I asked for it back once more, not expecting that to work, and again God gave it back to me.

In the end, my experience related to something I had learned through a book about Galatians. According to this book, Galatians focuses on whether people were trying to continue by means of the flesh when they had begun by means of the Spirit. If joy is a gift, a fruit of the Spirit's presence, there is no reason why God should not give it at any moment. It is not dependent on my persistence or failure but on God's giving. Not that I did nothing: I did sing praise songs on two or three occasions. But that would have gotten me nowhere without God's giving. And perhaps that is true for anyone, with joy or with whatever gift or fruit we would like. If we believe these things are God's gifts and not dependent on us, we might even ask God to give them to us.

There is a wonderful Glasgow band called the Blue Nile. They are perfectionists, and they release an album only once every six

years. The album in 1996 was called *Peace at Last*. The title track
asks the question, "Now that I've found peace at last, tell me Jesus,
will it last? Now that I've found peace of mind, tell me Jesus, is
it mine?" I've begun to believe that the answer might be yes. As
Habakkuk puts it, "Though the fig tree does not bud and there
are no grapes on the vines, though the olive crop fails and the
fields produce no food, though there are no sheep in the pen and
no cattle in the stalls, yet I will rejoice in the LORD, I will be joyful in God my Savior" (3:17–18)—if he gives me the gift.

On one of the occasions when I was in between joys, I felt
that nevertheless things were quite good with the world and in
that sense I was quite happy. But I told myself that this did not
count as joy in the Lord. It was just natural lightheartedness.

Then in the first week of term, we had a meditation in chapel
about the story of the woman anointing Jesus' feet, which provoked a Pharisee to query whether she had any business making an offering to Jesus. We were asked who the people were
who found fault with our offerings, and I knew that the only person who found fault with my offering was me. I did not think I
had anything worth offering. I knew this was wrong and that
although I did not believe in my gift to Jesus, he believed in it
and rejoiced in it. I did not know why I did not believe I had anything to offer Jesus that he would value, and at that moment I
did not know what my offering might be. Only a bit later did I
realize that my natural lightheartedness might be part of it. It
did not constitute joy, but if I gave it to God, it was transformed
into joy. It became the kind of rejoicing in the Lord of which
Philippians 4 speaks, and it was an offering Jesus was happy to
receive and consecrate. In general, I believe that spiritual gifts
and fruits are natural capacities released and brought to fulfillment and used to glorify Christ by the Spirit, and this was just
one example.

Then there was an occasion when I was running around our
sports field feeling joyful at 7:45 A.M. It was the day I was to take
Ann to the rehabilitation center for a stay—it was a scheduled
stay, not because there was a problem, though one did manage
to emerge. Yet as I was putting her into the car I found myself
crying, and I knew it was because that sort of moment brings
home to me the reality of her illness. Whereas we try to live a
"normal" life, a moment like that reminds me of the sadness of

how things actually are. That did not surprise me. What did surprise me was that juxtaposition of joy and tears. It should not have surprised me, because that is how our life is and how most human life is, I suspect. Quite often joy alternates with sadness. "Weeping may remain for a night, but rejoicing comes in the morning" (Ps. 30:5).

Some of us feel uncomfortable with the one, some with the other, some with both. If we are experiencing one, someone near us is bound to be experiencing the other. And maybe we then feel bad about the one we are experiencing, whether it is sadness or joy, or find it difficult to handle the fact that the other person is experiencing the opposite. God calls us to rejoice with those who rejoice and weep with those who weep, which may among other things mean that we are able to hold both together in ourselves, or at least to let them alternate rather than being unrealistically stuck in one or the other.

When I realized I did not believe that anything I could give Jesus was worthwhile, that he could be enthusiastic about anything I brought, I knew there was something more afoot than merely not being able to recognize the value of a particular gift. Behind my feeling was a more general uncertainty about me and God. I find it easy to identify with the woman who wanted merely to touch the edge of Jesus' coat to access the healing power and then hide so as not to cause too much trouble.

One morning when I was not especially thinking about this but was just having a quiet time, I was suddenly overwhelmed by joy as God pointed to something in me and in effect said, "Don't you see how I rejoice at that, at the way you give yourself to me in that." He was looking at me in love because I was doing my best in my feebleness, and I found myself in tears and in joy at the same time.

Joy is often like that, is it not? It involves tears because it brings out into the open your deepest fears, the anxieties you most hide from, which it can do because it confronts them and demonstrates that they are unfounded. Therefore, you can laugh and weep at the same time. You rejoice when things are tough, and you weep when things are great. The two are interwoven. When people returning from Babylon began to restore the temple, "No one could distinguish the sound of the shouts of joy from the sound of weeping" (Ezra 3:13) because they felt both sadness and joy. They do not just alternate. They are there at the same time.

So many things we achieve are achieved only through struggle and conflict, not in easy ways. They always seem to involve crosses. I have so longed to find somewhere in life some corner where joy is unmingled with pain. But I have never found it. Wherever I find joy, my own or other people's, it always seems to be mingled with pain. And I find that the people I most respect are people who know the link between joy and pain. And I have found that if we will own pain and weep over it together, we also find Christ's overflowing comfort. The bad news is that there may be no corner of reality where joy is not related to pain. The good news is that there is no corner of reality where pain cannot be transformed into overflowing joy.

Another thing occurred to me at about the same time. It had to do with the sequence in Galatians 5. "The fruit of the Spirit is love, joy, peace . . .". It suggests that joy flows from love. You might have thought that it flowed from being loved, and of course that is true. But Galatians opens up the other possibility—that joy flows from loving, from giving love.

God asks us to love people. You can give lots of yourself to one or two or three people. You can pour out yourself for them, like the woman with her bottle of perfume. The word *joy* is not in that story, but the story does indicate that because she poured herself out in love, she found forgiveness and salvation and peace, which are not unrelated to joy. Of course, she did not earn her forgiveness or her salvation that way. She was responding to the way Jesus had reached out to people and to what she knew was for her too. But it all became actual for her, the forgiveness and the salvation and the peace and the joy, because she gave the most precious thing she had in love.

In John 15, Jesus talks about love and joy, and in five verses he uses the word *love* eight times (vv. 9–13). In the middle of them he says, "I have told you this so that my joy may be in you and that your joy may be complete" (v. 11). His joy came from his loving, and so would theirs.

One Monday morning when Ann was going down with a bug, I woke up and found myself saying to God, "I do not trust you with Ann." Then before I could get struck by lightning I said,

"Well, in some ultimate sense I do trust you. I know it will be all right at the end. The problem is what you might let happen in the meantime." I have to let the trust that can hold for the end hold for the present. In other words, the fact that the Lord is at hand means that I can have a kind of anticipatory joy in the present when it is not the end.

In Philippians 4, it is not clear what Paul meant when he juxtaposed "Rejoice in the Lord always" (v. 4) with "the Lord is near" (v. 5). It is not clear what he sees as the link between the successive clauses. The Church of England reads this passage during Advent, which invites us to assume, plausibly, that Christ's second coming is a reason for joy in the now.

I mentioned in chapter 7 how I used to say that I would not mind if Rudolf Bultmann were correct and the second coming were a myth, but now I do mind. It matters that Jesus is going to finish the job he has begun, a job of putting down evil and restoring rightness. Both have been begun. Neither is finished. The Bible assumes that both will be reason for great joy when they are achieved, and that means we have reason for anticipatory joy now. I can trust God with Ann because I know God will finish.

10

Life

Death

I have mentioned the occasion when late one night while on a vacation in the Alps, two friends and I were discussing death. Two of us agreed that it was really quite an attractive prospect. It would be a relief. The third thought this was bizarre.

For me, it had something to do with being tired. The wonderful thing about this vacation was that it was a time when responsibilities were shed, burdens were shared, and furrows fell away from brows, and by the end I may not have felt the same about the attractiveness of death. I cannot remember. I do remember that it was hard to pick up the burdens and responsibilities again after that trip.

Death is entirely natural. There is a natural sequence that takes us from conception and birth through growth to maturity through senescence to death. It is not frightening or sad or incomplete. It is like a novel or a play with a beginning, a middle, and an end.

So what happens when we die? We do not cease to exist. We can see the person there, lying on a bed or somewhere. To be more dramatic, imagine a couple of teenagers, full of life, who lose control of their car on a bend and die. They still exist, but they are lifeless. They cannot move. As the Bible sees it, what happens to us inside is the same as what happens to us outside. Our personality still exists as our body still exists, but our personality becomes lifeless, energy-less, as our body does.

In traditional cultures, at least, people are laid to rest with their families. If we are buried in a family tomb, it will not be lonely there, but it will be dark and lifeless. We will be on the edge of the church. We will not be able to join in its worship as we once did. I once had to preach in a parish church and had to sit next to the tomb of Lady Newdigate, Countess of Derby, which had a sculpture of her recumbent form lying on the top. Two cherubic figures were shown praying in a space underneath her feet. Because she was a lady she was buried within reach of the communion table, but even she could not reach out and receive the bread and wine along with the living. She was present for the worship, but she could not join in. This is one of death's great deprivations, as the Bible sees it.

I love the poignant exposition of what death means in Ecclesiastes 9. The trouble is it brings out the downside to death, the way it makes you reevaluate the significance of life. Death is the great denial, the great nothingness.

Death is the place where there is no hope. In life you can keep hoping against hope, keep kidding yourself that there might be a change, keep praying. Where there is life, there is hope. Death is the great realism. There is not going to be healing. There is not going to be reconciliation. There is not going to be conversion. There is no hope. So even a living dog is better off than a dead lion (v. 4).

Death is the place where there is no knowledge (v. 5). The living know they will die; I am mortal, therefore I am. The dead know nothing.

And the dead are not known. Death is the place where people are forgotten (v. 5). Yes, there are exceptions. Plato and Aristotle are remembered, Amos and Jeremiah, Caesar and Brutus. But not the ordinary people who wrote out Plato and Aristotle's works and therefore made them available to us, not Amos's wife and Jeremiah's mother, not the people who cooked lunch for Caesar and Brutus, not the people like you and me. People say that one of the reasons people long to have children, or at least why they regret not having them, is that through children your name lives on, you live on. I discovered that a John Goldingay married an Ann Goldingay in Birmingham, where I come from, in 1842, exactly one hundred years before I was born. Now that I have written about them, they are not forgotten, but countless thousands of named and unnamed are forgotten.

Death is the place where people have no feelings: "Their love, their hate and their jealousy have long since vanished" (v. 6). Think of the massive, dynamic strength and significance of our loves, our hatreds, our jealousies, our wants, our passions, and our fury. They make us human. In death there will be none of them.

Death is the place where people can do nothing (v. 6). In life, we gain our significance from being able to take part in things, to contribute to discussions and arguments and decision making. "Where you are going, there is neither working nor planning nor knowledge nor wisdom" (v. 10).

And death is unpredictable. No one knows when his or her hour will come: "As fish are caught in a cruel net, or birds are taken in a snare, so [people] are trapped by evil times that fall unexpectedly upon them" (v. 12).

People sometimes talk as if this is merely the Old Testament understanding of death, by which they mean the Old Testament's (pardonable) misunderstanding, now corrected by the (true) New Testament understanding. But this Old Testament understanding is correct. One look in the tomb establishes it. The Christian instinctively says, "But that's just the body. The soul, the real person, is safe with God." And that is half true, but it is not enough. The body is as much the real person as the soul, and if the things the Bible says about death are true about the body, then they are true about the person. When resurrection comes, they will not be true, but for the time being, they are.

But I could relish all that. No more hoping (and therefore no more disappointment). No more knowing (and therefore no more knowing the tough things). No more feelings (and therefore no more worry about whether I am loved). No more doing (and therefore no more responsibility). Like endless Sunday.

But Ecclesiastes sees the negative side. What it says about death is true. "All share a common destiny—the righteous and the wicked, the good and the bad, the clean and the unclean, those who offer sacrifices and those who do not" (v. 2). So what is the point of being righteous, good, clean, worshipful?

They are worthwhile in their own right. Death does not stop them from being so. But it does underline a problem. What if that sequence of birth-growth-maturity-senescence-death does not work out in that neat way? I have referred more than once to a time when I would not have been bothered if being raised from the dead to new life in heaven were a myth. I would have enjoyed my life, it would have had its own plot, its own beginning, middle, and end, and I would have been happy enough to bow out when the curtain dropped. That is still to some extent true, but only to some extent. I am more aware now of the force of Jesus' argument in Mark 12:18–27, where he grounds the necessity of resurrection in the fact that God is the God of the living, not of the dead. One of the implications is that when God enters into a relationship with people such as Abraham, Isaac, or Jacob, or you or me, that is not likely to be a temporary affair. God does not give up on relationships like that. For Ann and me, each time we have said good-bye to someone who has mattered to us, it has been like another little death. We are who we are because of our friendships with these people, so a bit of us dies when these friendships die in their present form. God is not going to let us die like that.

But Ecclesiastes reminds me of another reason why I am less easygoing about the resurrection from the dead. It is one of the reasons for the development of belief in the resurrection within Judaism. If the resurrection is not a reality, things are unfair. Dan Cohn-Sherbock has argued in his book *Holocaust Theology* that belief in a resurrection is essential if Jews are to make sense of the fact of the Holocaust.[1] In so arguing, he is repeating the logic that drove many Jewish people to this belief two millennia ago, beginning with the visions in Daniel. In my case, belief in the resurrection has important links with Ann in particular. It is important to me that, though confined to a wheelchair now, she will dance in heaven. I respect the author of Ecclesiastes for living a tough faith without that conviction; Jews in his day had no empirical evidence for it and would not have any such evidence until Jesus rose from the dead. I am glad I live on the other side of that resurrection, even though believing in Ann's and mine is still a matter of faith.

There is another aspect to the way we experience death. In one sense, in theory, there is a clear distinction between life and death.

I have watched only one person die: Ann's mother. It was itself both strange and providential. As Ann's mother grew older and passed into her eighties, we wondered how the end might eventually come. We also wondered how we might cope with her increasing frailness, as she lived two hours' drive away and Ann was herself disabled. She came to stay with us one Christmas as usual, and between Christmas and New Year we went to see the film *When Harry Met Sally*. Halfway through, to my annoyance, she felt sick, and we had to leave the cinema and go home. Eventually, it became clear that she had had a heart attack. At first she seemed to improve, but on New Year's Day, the hospital called to suggest we come in. By the time we reached her bedside, she was unconscious, and we sat there for some time—I cannot remember how long. She was breathing quite loudly, almost snoring. Then I remember a moment when she simply stopped. And I remember thinking, "That's it." That was life; this is death.

Yet in another sense life and death overlap and interweave. We talk about feeling deathly. We get the flu and lie in bed not moving or speaking or eating for a day or two and not wishing to talk to anyone, and it is like a little death. We are for a while overwhelmed by fears or depressions or responsibilities or guilts or hatreds, and it is like having the soil fall onto the coffin as you lie there in the newly dug grave. Or you say all those good-byes, and you feel you are losing part of what made you alive.

It is as if death has got hold of us while we are still alive. And this is how the Bible sees it. Many of the psalms speak of being in Sheol, the corporate grave that is the nonmaterial equivalent to the material tomb, or they speak of having been rescued from Sheol when people were delivered from illness or depression or danger. They speak of being overwhelmed by floods, which are the waters of death. Life and death interweave all right. It reminds me of the lines in T. S. Eliot's poem "Journey of the Magi" in which one of the wise men wonders about the link between birth and death and realizes that being involved with Christ's birth has taken them through a kind of death, for things that previously suggested life have now died. "I should be glad of another death," he comments. Is life attractive, or is death attractive?

Life

But what difference does it make that Jesus came back from death to begin a transformed life? Let me relate it to three things that happened when we visited California in connection with the possibility of moving there.

Just beforehand, in the southwestern tip of California, thirty-nine people committed suicide, believing that the Hale-Bopp comet was a sign that God was coming to take them to be with him. One may be astonished that people should believe anything so certain that it is worth dying for. From a Christian angle, what is odd is not the fact of the certainty but the lack of a basis for it. The fact of the certainty might make us ask how convinced we ourselves are about matters of life and death. A person who had left the cult told the newspapers, "We were seekers of what was going on, why we were here, what the purpose of life is." These people were not crazy Californians, except by adoption. They were people from Ohio and Connecticut who had gone to California on a spiritual pilgrimage, in what the newspaper called "the great American temptation." It was a continuation of what brought people to the New World in the first place.

At about the same time, the film *The English Patient* received an Oscar. It is the story of a man who has been horrifically injured in an airplane accident in North Africa during World War II. He lies encased in bandages, unable to move. In due course, an enemy catches up with him but declines to kill him because that would actually be an act of mercy. The man is waiting to die, but in another sense, he says, "I died ages ago." He is referring not merely to the near death of his accident but to an event that preceded that, when he lost the only woman he had loved.

While we were in California, we were shown some houses by a realtor. Now, as a Church of England minister, I had never bought a house before and thus had little experience with realtors. My impression of them was that they were people who would tell any lie to make a sale. Our realtor subverted that slanderous impression. She loved people and she loved property, and she seemed to gain her fulfillment from putting the right property and the right people together.

The week we met her was the week after Easter, and she happened to express her anger at the sermon she had heard on Easter Day, a sermon that was geared to children and the television generation. It had taken up some C. S. Lewis story that perhaps expressed the gospel (indeed, as it was Lewis, no doubt it expressed the gospel), but for her it failed to focus clearly enough on the fact that Jesus was alive.

I was struck by the fierceness of her feelings on this matter and a bit puzzled by them. The next day while we were out looking at some more properties, I discovered the background for her anger. Eight years previously her eighteen-year-old son had gone for a drive in the mountains that tower above Pasadena, had failed to make a bend, and had plunged to the bottom of a ravine. This had happened at about the time when faith in Christ was becoming a reality to her. Her son's death did not lead her to Christ, nor did it drive her away from Christ, but it did somehow come to constitute one of the key factors in determining what Christ meant for her. She did not quite articulate what this was, but I think it had to do with the fact that because Christ rose to new life, somehow it was possible to live with her son's death. It gave her hope. And that was why she was so angry that the Easter sermon had not focused explicitly on the fact that Jesus was alive.

She makes me think again of the ending of Job's story, when Job gets reestablished with his new life and his new family. I find that students do not like the story's ending; it is too neat and unrealistic, they feel. They prefer the tough realism of the protesting Job. But theologically and pastorally the story's ending promises us that stories do have endings, that our story will have an ending. They do not finish with families decimated, lovers dead, and lives broken and empty. The story of Job is realistic for theological reasons that are based in the nature of God but are given grounds by the resurrection of Jesus. Easter means that our stories will have an ending.

There was another fact about Easter that came home to me that week. It is a solemn fact that ministry can often seem a deathly business. "We are hard pressed . . . perplexed . . . persecuted . . . struck down" in the course of our ministry, says Paul. "We always carry around in our body the death of Jesus" (2 Cor. 4:8–10). Yes, death is not something that waits until we die. Easter means we die with Christ, but it also means we live with Christ. I heard a sermon that drew attention to the fact that when Mary thought Jesus was the gardener, she was not wrong. He was not only the firstfruits of the dead but the gardener producing fruit.

11

Love

"Love your neighbor as yourself" (Lev. 19:18). It is a rather ambiguous exhortation. In recent decades, it has been understood to mean, "Love your neighbor as you love yourself," and it has become a proof-text of the notion of "loving oneself" as a key to personal health. It is the only such proof-text as far as I know. I cannot think of other Scripture passages that explicitly encourage us to love ourselves or accept ourselves as we are, though I can think of a few that seem to suggest the opposite.

It might be hypothesized that the cultures of the Bible were healthier than ours, that the notion (or rather the reality) of accepting oneself could be taken for granted. But I am generally wary of arguments that suggest that people in the Bible were different from us as human beings. In other connections, it is important for us to assume that they were quite like us, and that assumption proves fruitful. It seems at least as likely that our preoccupation with ourselves needs to be confronted rather than accepted. The Bible's emphasis on giving your life away and getting it back as a result provides a different way into the issues involved in the notion of loving oneself. Perhaps we will find more acceptance of ourselves and love for ourselves through giving ourselves to others than in focusing on loving ourselves. Further, it is uncertain whether "Love your neighbor as yourself" means what has been suggested. It is more likely to mean, "You shall love your neighbor as a person like yourself."

What is love? The companion exhortation about loving God may give us clues. We are to love God with all our heart, soul, and strength (Deut. 6:5), with all our heart, soul, and mind (Matt. 22:37), with all our heart, soul, mind, and strength (Mark 12:30). The variation reflects differences in the connotations of some of these words. In Hebrew the "heart" denotes what we would call the workings of the mind rather than the emotions, for which you would more likely refer to lower parts of the anatomy (we too speak of a fluttering in the tummy). What each of these forms of expression makes clear is that love for God requires the whole person—mind, feelings, will, and energy. It is a reaching out and committing oneself on the part of the whole person.

Loving another human being is the same. It too involves reaching out in commitment, reaching out with affection and consideration, reaching out by thinking of them and seeking to understand them and thinking the best of them, reaching out by spending time and money and energy and life. It involves the whole person given to someone else. That is how God's love for us is. God thinks the best of us, wants to understand us, and likes to hear from us in order to develop that process. God gives everything for us, even the only son God had.

Love is thus a demanding business, even a painful business. That feeling in the pit of the stomach is as likely to be an anxious pain as an excited flutter. This is true of romantic love but also of other forms of love. The point is well expressed in Hannah Hurnard's allegory of love, *Hinds' Feet on High Places*. The hero, Much-Afraid, shrinks back from having the seed of Love planted in her heart. "I am afraid. . . . I have been told that if you really love someone you give that loved one the power to hurt and pain you in a way nothing else can."[1] The Shepherd's response affirms the truth of her statement but adds that there is happiness in love even if you are not loved in return. Yet he promises that when Love is ready to bloom in her heart and when she is ready to change her name, she will in fact be loved in return. He offers her the seed of Love.

She bent forward to look, then gave a startled little cry and drew
back. There was indeed a seed . . . but it was shaped exactly like
a long, sharply pointed thorn. Much-Afraid had often noticed that
the Shepherd's hands were scarred and wounded, but now she
saw that the scar in the palm of the hand held out to her was the
exact shape and size of the seed of Love lying beside it.[2]

The Shepherd reminds her that "Love and Pain go together, for
a time at least. If you would know Love, you must know pain
too."[3]

It is not a uniquely Christian insight. Richard Olivier comments in *Shadow of the Stone Heart*, "I was learning the hard
way you can't just increase the capacity to love without simultaneously increasing the propensity for pain."[4] But he was determined that he would no longer sacrifice the feelings of love and
joy because they involved owning the feelings of pain and loss.
"As someone once said, 'It is important that when Death finds
you, it finds you alive.'"[5]

It is easy for love to be self-centered. It is easy to be at least
as interested in the love we get in return for giving love as in the
mere giving of the love itself. Real love gains its happiness from
the giving, not the anticipated or actual reciprocation. It is a little like artistic creativity. The painter or sculptor or musician
may not care whether anyone appreciates his or her work; that
is not the point. The point is to have created something true.

So it is with love. Its point is to have done something true,
even if the object of love makes no response. (Of course, we know
that there is a response of love from God, whose heart thrills
with delight because we have loved.)

In due course, Much-Afraid reaches an exalted place, dominated by a mighty waterfall, whose waters leap down from a
height high above her and her two companions, Sorrow and Suffering. The Shepherd asks Much-Afraid:

> "What do you think of this fall of great waters in their abandon-
> ment of self-giving?" She trembled a little as she answered, "I
> think they are beautiful and terrible beyond anything which I ever
> saw before." "Why terrible?" he asked. "It is the leap which they
> have to make, the awful height from which they must cast them-
> selves down to the depths beneath, there to be broken on the
> rocks. I can hardly bear to watch it." "Look closer," he said again.

"Let your eye follow just one part of the water from the moment when it leaps over the edge until it reaches the bottom." Much-Afraid did so, and then almost gasped with wonder. Once over the edge, the waters were like winged things, alive with joy, so utterly abandoned to the ecstasy of giving themselves that she could almost have supposed that she was looking at a host of angels floating down on rainbow wings, singing with rapture as they went. She gazed and gazed, then said, "It looks as though they think it is the loveliest moment in all the world, as though to cast oneself down is to abandon oneself to ecstasy and joy inde-scribable." . . . The lower the water fell, the lighter it seemed to grow, as though it really were lighting down on wings. On reach-ing the rocks below, all the waters flowed together in a glorious host, forming an exuberant, rushing torrent which swirled tri-umphantly around and over the rocks. Laughing and shouting at the top of their voices, they hurried still lower and lower, down through the meadows to the next precipice and the next glorious crisis of their self-giving.[6]

"There is nothing love cannot face; there is no limit to its faith, its hope, and its endurance." So says the New English Bible's version of 1 Corinthians 13:7. It is tempting to think that there are many things love cannot face. When you have done some-thing wrong by someone you love, you may naturally and rightly fear telling that person. You are not sure his or her love can face it. We once knew a woman who had had an abortion some years ago. She had not told any of the friends she had made since she had come to faith in Christ, because she feared her act would destroy their picture of her (or their love for her) as the joyful dedicated Christian she was.

If our relationship with God were based on God not knowing some things about us, that would imperil the relationship. It would make it unreal. The more committed a relationship is, the more important it seems that we should be able to say any-thing in its context, and in particular, that we should be able to share the shameful things. Otherwise, apparent depth in the relationship turns out to be based on falsehood.

God's love can face things. Worthwhile love on the part of other human beings is like that too; their love can face things. And for us to love involves being like that ourselves. We can face

things in other people and thereby bring them a new form of
freedom.

① There is no limit to love's faith, to its capacity to believe in
the other person. God demonstrated an extraordinary faith in
Israel and in what it could be and achieve, like the belief a mother
has in her children or a wife has in her husband. Indeed, both
the analogy of parenthood and that of marriage appear in Israel's
story. Then Jesus tells eleven members of Israel that he is entrusting them with the task of discipling all the nations. A midrash
tells of Jesus announcing this plan to the angels ahead of time.
One of them asks what his backup plan is if this one fails. "I have
no other plan," Jesus says. That is the degree of his faith in them,
his trust in them. Our love for people involves a similar trust, a
belief that may make it possible for them to do things they could
not otherwise do.

② There is also no limit to love's hope. God had a vision for
Israel, the way a mother has a vision for her children. The story
in Hosea 11 draws painful attention to the way a mother's vision
may be long unfulfilled but not abandoned. God has a vision for
us and is not yet finished with us. That is a powerful stimulus
to change for us. And we have a vision for people we love. But
there is a difference between having a vision of what we wish
another person to be and having a vision of what that person
could be, a vision that sees the realization of potentials. We may
be able to hope for them what they could not hope for themselves. There is no limit to love's hope.

③ And there is no limit to its endurance. Again, we can see this
is so as we consider the story of God's relationship with Israel
or with the church, and again the comparison with a mother is
an instructive one. The picture in Hosea 11 presupposes that a
mother's endurance is never exhausted. An Old Testament colleague who is a mother talks about the fact that no matter what
her sons do, no matter how exasperated or angry with them she
might become, she could never cease being their mother. She
in one sense looks forward to the time when they will leave home
to live their lives as adults, but she could never throw them out
because they had finally crossed a line. There is no limit to the
endurance of love. Our love for each other will persist.

As the time of our departure from England drew near, I went
to a farewell lunch with some of our students. Toward the end

one delivered a touching speech. "You have too big a love for St. John's Theological College," he said, "and I am afraid that your love will be too big for Fuller Seminary." I did not know what he meant, but it sounded nice, and I wanted to think about it and consider whether it was some form of word from God. Then I realized that actually he had said, "You have too big a laugh for St. John's Theological College, and I am afraid your laugh will be too big for Fuller Seminary."

But the notions of a "big love" and "too big a love" bear thinking about. It is a big love that can face anything and that has no end to its faith, its hope, and its endurance. And too big a love overflows and spills out to others.

For his book on religion and rock, Steve Turner took his title from Bruce Springsteen's song "Hungry for Heaven." Turner's thesis is that the restlessness expressed in rock music and usually focused on human relationships is the same restlessness that Augustine speaks of, one that reaches out farther than it realizes. The live version of "Hungry Heart" on Springsteen's retrospective compilation of live performances shows why music is a live business: He leaves the audience quite alone to do the singing at the beginning. Springsteen sings the story of someone who has kept seeking the fulfillment of his heart's longing and in the course of doing so has never found a place to rest, a home. "Everybody's got a hungry heart."

I was once struck by a few lines of a track on Jeff Buckley's album *Grace*. It is the story of a Bible character, David, a man with much more ambiguity in his life than the plaster saint portrayals usually allow. In the song, David is the baffled king, singing hallelujah but no longer understanding God, beguiled by a woman and letting her break his throne in return for the joy she brought him, proving that love is "a cold and . . . a broken hallelujah."

The lines simultaneously and devastatingly question the reality of human relationships and of relationships with God and thus bring out into the open the secret dreads and doubts about God and other loves that we dare not name even to ourselves. If we doubt God, we cannot take refuge in the fact that at least a human love is secure. If we are not sure of human love, neither can we take refuge in the conviction that God's love is "safe."

The song is by Leonard Cohen, the Canadian Jewish writer and composer who often takes up religious themes in such a way as this, though nowhere else as disturbingly, I would say. Jennifer Warnes, who was once a backup singer for Cohen and who has herself recorded an album of his songs, said that the great thing about Cohen was that he said the things no one else would say.

In the spring of 1997, Jeff Buckley, who had made the definitive recording of this song, walked into the Mississippi and drowned, dragged into an undertow by a riverboat. First accounts said he was playing his guitar, which seemed bizarre. A later version reported more plausibly that as he went in for a swim he was singing Led Zeppelin's "Whole Lotta Love" as it played on a ghetto blaster. He was just past the age at which his singer father, Tim Buckley, whom he had hardly met, had died of drugs.

I have suggested that Meat Loaf's "Bat out of Hell" (itself a love song) illustrates how Jim Steinman's songs and arrangements are written as if for fun but deceive you because they often conceal a sting or a sadness in the tale. My next favorite to "Bat out of Hell" is "Two out of Three Ain't Bad": "I need you, I want you, but there ain't no way I'm ever gonna love you." It sounds stereotypically male. But as you listen to the song it turns out that he cannot let himself love because of his experience of being broken by the woman who he thought loved him and who said those words to him.

My favorite film of 1995 was *Leaving Las Vegas*, the story of an alcoholic writer who goes to Las Vegas to drink himself to death. There he meets a prostitute, and they fall in love. He dies loved, while she goes into the rest of her life having loved. Someone who came to see it with Ann and me was puzzled as to why a Christian wanted to see such a gloomy film. For me it was an encouraging film because it looked the grimmest of experiences in the eye and declared that if there is love, it is possible to die and it is also possible to live on (better to have loved and lost . . .).

About the same time we went to see *Sense and Sensibility*, toward which I have a certain antipathy. The story involves the threat that two women will lose the men they love. Twenty minutes before the end I thought and hoped it was going to turn out like that, with the two sisters then proving that it was possible to live on with each other's sisterly friendship. But in those last few minutes, everything got sorted out and the sisters were able to marry happily.

We were discussing the two films with friends, and I was saying how much I preferred *Leaving Las Vegas*. One of the friends who knew me too well commented, "Yes, you would go for doomed romance." I protested that it was romanced doom that I went for (i.e., gloom tempered by romance), but later I realized that the comment was correct. I like the idea suggested by *Leaving Las Vegas* that even if love is doomed and it is necessary to live on anyway, this is possible. But I can believe that only because God is real and therefore Leonard Cohen's awful vision can be looked in the face but not seen as the final word.

12

Realism

Jesus once told an extraordinary story about a farm manager. The farm owner gave the manager a formal warning because he was dissatisfied with the manager's work performance. This galvanized him into action. He summoned the owner's creditors and told them that if they paid now, he would settle for half the amount they owed. At least that would mean he had "friends" when he lost his job. When the owner discovered what had happened, he was unable to conceal his admiration for the manager's shrewdness.

There is a British organization called the Scripture Union that among other things publishes notes to help people understand the Bible. The organization has a logo consisting of an oil lamp, recalling the verse in Psalms that describes God's Word as a lamp to illuminate the way for us. Years ago I heard someone suggest that if the logo was ever redesigned, it ought to be changed to a pair of raised eyebrows, because the Bible is always saying things that surprise us. It is never predictable or boring. The parables are best of all at such surprises. In another parable, a widow makes a terrible nuisance of herself with a judge, who eventually sees that justice is done only because this is the one way to get the wretched woman off his back. The story serves as an example of prayer. Then there is the one about the Publican and the Pharisee. Think of the Publican as an embodiment of the Thatcherite/Reaganite enterprise economy; think of the Pharisee as the committed churchman, concerned to see Scripture embodied in his life and the lives of others. Who goes home right with God? Not the Pharisee. Or what about the man who gets mugged on the way to Jericho and is ignored by a professor and a hospital chaplain but gets cared for by a Samaritan?

Why are Jesus' parables so extraordinary, so eyebrow-raising? There are various reasons, but what lies behind them is the fact that the gospel Jesus is and that he brings is so important but so extraordinary that eyebrow-raising stories are needed to convey it.

Jesus told the story of the shrewd manager to shake people out of torpor into action. Jesus' coming meant that the crucial moment in his people's history was dawning—indeed, the crucial moment in world history was dawning. He had come to bring new life to Israel and to the world. What attitude people took in regard to Jesus would make a decisive difference in regard to their destiny. Could they recognize that the decisive moment had arrived, that their number was up?

Perhaps the parable reminds us of moments in politics. Indeed, there are close parallels between party politics and the shrewd manager: Does not his story remind you of some politician distributing largesse on the eve of an election, in the conviction that that is the way to buy reelection from the voters?

There are also moments like that in our personal lives. This is one of the themes in the film *Dead Poets Society*, a marvelous if rather pagan story about young men discovering who they are and trying not to conform to the expectations of parents and other despised species. One of them meets the girl of his dreams and to woo her has to take action that is dangerously and amusingly bold, given that she is already nearly engaged to a large football-playing gentleman. Another throws himself into acting despite his father's insistence that he is destined to be a doctor. They cannot let life simply wash over them if they are to do what they have to do. They have to make decisions, take action.

Just after this parable Luke conveys words of Jesus that comprise a challenge to a decision. "No servant can serve two masters" (Luke 16:13). You have to choose between God and Mammon. An American seminary professor gets paid less than a pastor but more than a British seminary professor or pastor. What will serving Christ mean now? How will I live with money and God? How do we use worldly wealth in a way that brings us nearer an eternal home (Luke 16:9)? Many people no doubt wish that wealth was their problem, instead of the problem of making ends meet. But all of us have to face a decision regarding God or Mammon, a broad gate or a narrow one through which we need to walk if we are to join the few who find life. It does not happen accidentally. It does not happen if you simply drift. That, says Jesus, is the broad way that leads nowhere or worse.

Jesus did not just bring a crisis and a challenge to first-century people, scribes and fishermen and zealots and whores and priests and tax collectors and other characters. He was the decisive person in world history, and he still is. "Don't be so stupid that you fail to recognize a decisive moment when it arrives," says Jesus.

Facing the Facts as a Community

The date is October 17. The year 520 B.C. It is the last day of the Feast of Tabernacles, Israel's great festival at the end of the farming year, one of the occasions when people came to Jerusalem on pilgrimage. People camped together for a week and looked back over what God had done for them and wondered what the new year would bring.

There is a special significance about this particular year in the history of the people of God, and God sends Haggai to them with a special message, recorded in Haggai 2:1–9. Like a typical prophet Haggai points the people to some facts about past, present, and future to bring them promises and challenges.

He wants them to face the real facts about the present. At the Feast of Tabernacles they might be able to avoid facing these facts. After all, the festival was designed to remind the people of the wonder of their deliverance from Egypt. If they are celebrating God's acts, they might be averting their eyes from the realities of the present.

Haggai gently draws attention to the contrast between past and present and invites them to own it. He reminds them of the fact that their days of glory lie in the past. There was once a day when Davidic kings ruled in Jerusalem. They had real kings then—all they have now is Zerubbabel the son of Shealtiel. His genealogy marks him as a person who could be king if there were a king, but in this situation he is only a "governor" appointed by the Persians.

There was once a day when they had quality high priests, people whose position no one would query. All they have now is Joshua the son of Jehozadak, and we know from Zechariah 3 that he was disparaged (by members of the local population who had not been in exile) for being tainted by the impurity of exile.

There was once a day when they were a real people, an entity to be reckoned with in Middle Eastern politics and history. All they are now is a "remnant." We know what a remnant is—the leftover bits of wallpaper or material that a store sells off cheaply.

Haggai particularly notes that they had a real temple then, one that puts to shame the temple the community is trying to build. Its shape may be the same, but it does not contain the covenant chest and the covenant stones, the cherubim, the pot of manna, Aaron's rod, the urim and thummim, the imported wooden paneling, the gold. . . . People who were old enough to have known the first temple (they would have had to be over seventy!) wept when they saw the second (see Ezra 3; Ezra 1–6 tells the story that provides the context for the work of Haggai and Zechariah).

Facing facts is difficult. That is true of individuals: Doctors and relatives find it difficult to tell someone he or she has a terminal disease. It is true of a nation: A country such as Britain finds it difficult to come to terms with its reduced significance in the world. It is true of the church: It is tempting to hide from the fact that the church is in decline. How can you face facts?

Haggai believes that the key is to consider the invisible facts about the present. In his first prophecy, he was rather confrontational in rebuking them about their commitment to God. Here he wants to be encouraging. "I am with you—be strong,

says Yahweh Sebaot." That phrase is Haggai's special title for
God. English translations have "the LORD Almighty," which
waters it down. The name means "Yahweh Armies." It expresses
concretely and vividly the power of God, which is what the people need to believe in.

The hidden facts about God in the present provide a context
in which we face facts about an individual's illness, or about a
nation that has lost an empire and not found a role, or about a
church in decline. Hope lies not in doctrinal soundness or trendi-
ness or social involvement or the latest charisms. Haggai's
encouragement is God. The resource of the church is God active
in a hidden way, building up the people of God as a temple of
the Spirit.

As well as facing the facts about the past and the hidden facts
about the present, Haggai wants them to look at the guaranteed
facts about the future. Faith means being sure of what we hope
for and certain of what we do not see (Heb. 11:1). "I will fill this
house with glory," God says (Hag. 2:7). The recurrent word in
Haggai's vision of their future is *glory*. Glory suggests the outward visible splendor of a monarch in state robes. It is not the
nature of their present experience.

For Israel it will mean "prosperity" (RSV) or "peace" (NIV). Both
aspects of the meaning of *shalom* are surely appropriate (REB).
Yet what Haggai promises will come about for God's glory not
merely for Israel's sake. All the world will come to worship at
the throne of the king.

It will come about by God's act—it was God who filled the
temple with glory before, and it will be God who does so again.
Human beings cannot make that happen. It will come "in a little while." It is imminent because it is dependent only on God's
acting. It will come about as part of a final reordering of all
things. It will involve a great "shaking" like the shaking at the
exodus and at Sinai (cf. Heb. 12:25–27).

As with many promises in Scripture, the final reordering did
not come in the prophet's day, but something did, a kind of fore-
taste of the final fulfillment of God's promise (see Ezra 6 regarding how things turned out). So it often is with healing and with
peace among the nations and with renewal in the church. We
have to ask for them as gifts that belong to the End. They will
become full reality only in connection with the End. But we have

to look for the foretastes that may be what we get in the meantime, and rejoice in these for what they are and for what they promise.

The facts about the future are guaranteed by the word of Yahweh Armies, Almighty God (five times in Hag. 2:6–9). When God speaks, things happen.

Limitations

I love Ecclesiastes. Actually, I love all of the Old Testament. I have friends who belong to the New Testament Church of God in Britain. I always say I belong to the Old Testament Church of God. One of the things I love about it is the way it interacts with human life as it is. The book that does that most systematically is Ecclesiastes.

The name is Greek; it means "church member" or "church leader." That corresponds to the book's Hebrew name, Qohelet, which has the same meaning. The opening verse of the book thus describes what follows as the words of the "teacher" or "preacher." It then identifies him as the son of David and king in Jerusalem, which enhances the book's authority, because it means this is a book of wisdom like the Proverbs "of Solomon" or the Song of Songs "of Solomon."

After that it may be surprising to find that the opening words of Solomon's teaching are "Meaningless! Meaningless! . . . Utterly meaningless! Everything is meaningless!" (1:2). It turns out that there is another significance in the opening verse in regard to Solomon. Solomon was the man who had everything, so if there were ever a man who had the chance to find what he was looking for, it was Solomon. Solomon stands for the use of the mind, but he acknowledges that the more he has discovered intellectually, the more grief he has felt. He has asked many questions but not found many answers. Solomon stands for enjoyment, but his story shows that it turned to dust in his mouth. Solomon stands for achievement; he is the man who built the temple and made Jerusalem what it was. But that has turned into dust in his mouth as well. It is meaningless. The word literally means a "breath."

Christians are inclined to stand superior in relation to Ecclesiastes. It may seem to resemble the darkness into which the gospel in due course will shine more than the light of the gospel itself. Yet when we talk this way, we may be hiding from the reality of how Christian life is, for Christians work at intellectual questions such as the meaning of suffering and do not know the answers. Christians try to get to the top of the ladder in their profession, try to win architectural competitions and to get into the final at Wimbledon and to make a hit album and to get elected to Congress. And some succeed. And they find that these achievements turn to dust in their mouths.

Indeed, there is more. In a telling observation, the Teacher describes how "[God] has made everything beautiful in its time. He has also set eternity in the hearts of [people]; yet they cannot fathom what God has done from beginning to end" (3:11). That has not changed. And the problem is not merely intellectual. The Teacher has seen something else. Where there ought to be just judgment, there is wickedness (3:16). The Teacher has seen the oppression that takes place in the world (another irony here, for the historical Solomon was a major cause of it in his own country): "I saw the tears of the oppressed—and they have no comforter; power was on the side of their oppressors—and they have no comforter" (4:1). Page after page of this realism confronts us, rubbing our noses in the realities of human experience that affect believers as they do unbelievers.

The conclusion is then surprising: People can do nothing better than to eat and drink and find satisfaction in their work. That comes from God. It is God's gift (3:22). A portrait of God as the great giver is the surprising center to the theology of Ecclesiastes. We feel a tension between the exposure of all pretension to understand or make sense of life and the bold and stark invitation to hold faith in God the giver, but it sets before us a vision preferable to the alternatives. What are these alternatives? To pretend that the question is not there and that everything can be solved in Christ. That is the usual Christian ploy. To pretend that the question is not there and that we can find meaning in fame or achievement or whatever. That is the usual non-Christian ploy. I prefer Ecclesiastes' invitation to realism and trust.

Ecclesiastes in Southern California

I live in a society characterized by a relentless activism. Christians as much as anyone else spend their lives rushing around ceaselessly on the freeway and continually doing business on their cell phones. "What do they gain from it all?" Ecclesiastes asks. Relentlessly, they pursue new experiences—new music, new films, new fashions, new holiday destinations, new mission opportunities. "The eye never has enough of seeing, nor the ear its fill of hearing," Ecclesiastes observes (1:8). If in due course they collapse in front of the television, the advertisements inexorably promise them something new—a new car, a new hamburger, a new computer, an all-new episode of the series that follows. But "there is nothing new under the sun," Ecclesiastes comments (1:9). Their society through no fault of its own has no past, though it longs for one, and it has no way of knowing what it might look like in the future. "There is no remembrance of [the people] of old, and even those who are yet to come will not be remembered," Ecclesiastes reflects (1:11).

Southern California is the society where Western civilization is tested to destruction, so the rest of the West had better pay attention to how the experiment is going. The West in general lives by the myth of progress. Because technology advances, therefore humanity has progressed. Now, I am grateful for the invention of the flush toilet, but it is difficult for us to acknowledge that in most areas that matter, humanity has made no progress over the millennia. Ecclesiastes offers to deliver us from our self-deception.

The Solomon of Ecclesiastes was the original Southern Californian. He tried everything. He can testify from experience concerning matters that ordinary people can only speculate about. In addition, he was the great philosopher. He thought as well as acted. That, too, should enable him to reflect on human experience in an instructive way.

His testimony confirms that our vast human activism cannot achieve things that matter or put right the real problems of the world. The country that can put a man on the moon cannot solve the problems of poverty, prejudice, and inequality in its backyard. The society that puts a huge emphasis on research into psychological and social problems cannot enable people to find happiness. The logical result is to be quite disillusioned with the notion of research.

Solomon's great experiment does not make him conclude that research, work, and relaxation are pointless. They are indeed *absolutely* pointless, but they are nevertheless *relatively* worthwhile. They cannot provide ultimate answers or fulfillment, but they can provide something.

One of the foundations of modernity was the attempt to discover ultimate answers by starting from scratch rather than from supposed "divine revelation." Descartes thus began from "I think, therefore I am." But the subsequent history of thought has established that philosophy cannot generate answers to ultimate questions. In that sense, wisdom is useless. Yet wisdom still excels folly as light excels darkness. It is *absolutely* useless but *relatively* useful.

One way we seek to find meaning is through work, but our work is also *ultimately* meaningless. Who knows how our successors will carry it on, whether they will ignore it or undo it or prove it wrong? Secondhand bookshops and university library stacks are full of the dusty, now-unread writings of nineteenth-century biblical scholars, and the works on which I labor will soon join them. But our work is *relatively* useful. Perhaps my writing these lines may help someone see how Ecclesiastes impacts his or her life. That is not nothing.

We cannot start from ourselves and reach the awareness that God is there. But if we start from the awareness that God is there, that changes the way we look at our lives and the little things that give meaning to them. And the conviction that God is there and is the source of life's pleasures is a reasonable conviction. God has not given us the answers to many of the big questions, but God has not given us nothing.

"There is a time for everything," Ecclesiastes goes on (3:1). When the Byrds made this poem a top ten hit in the 1960s, the idea that there was an appropriate or necessary time for life's activities and experiences presumably came across as a comfort. Ecclesiastes' subsequent comments about times fit with that idea, though they qualify it in a way consistent with Solomon's testimony. Yes, all these human experiences have their time. But what is the framework in which they all fit? God has not told us.

It is a clearly postmodern point in a quintessentially postmodern book. We cannot know the nature of the big picture into which everything fits. But perceiving the nature of the little pictures that make up life is not to be despised.

One of Ecclesiastes' recurrent themes is money. It acknowledges that money is important but urges that it is less important than people think. It is strangely deceptive or strangely unfulfilling. A current television advertisement acknowledges that the most precious things in life are priceless, but for all the rest we have a certain credit card. We decline to acknowledge that more money and things will do us no good, and as a result, we are inhibited from enabling some poor people (for whom a little more could make a huge difference) to have that little more. The sensible thing is to enjoy the good things of life that God gives, without pretending that they can provide ultimate satisfaction or meaning.

We received a Christmas card from one of Ann's former psychotherapy patients who remembers the sessions she had with Ann and looks back on them as a decisive shaping influence on her life. Today, Ann cannot remember what country she lives in, nor what day it is, nor the names of the two caregivers who have helped look after her for four years, nor the name of the grandson who brought her such joy when he was here last year. She cannot swallow or speak. She will watch the television news, though I am not sure how much she takes in.

On that news one day, we were hearing of the terrible cost of the Russian invasion of Chechnya, of the suffering of the local people. The pictures were too grim to show us. That afternoon I took her out for a walk in her wheelchair in the warm January sun, as I often do. As I pushed her back up the hill to our condo, I sang silly songs and pretended I was not going to make it to the top, and she laughed. It is not enough, but it is not nothing, and it is certainly not to be despised. It is a gift from God. That is what Ecclesiastes says.

It is also a wonderful gift from God that Ecclesiastes should be in the canon of Scripture. I cannot imagine how it got through some community screening procedure. Actually, I can. I think they were overcome by the truth it speaks.

13

Remembering

As Moses is about to give up the leadership of Israel, as the Old Testament tells the story, he preaches one last sermon. He has led the Israelites for a generation, and they are now about to enter a new stage of life. God has made it clear that this new stage, which will see the fulfillment of God's vision, will happen under a new leader. Moses can look on the land where God's vision will take the Israelites, but he will not walk in it with them. He is about to undertake a new journey of his own, and the mountain he is about to climb has some surprises in store for him.

So on the eve of climbing the mountain, he preaches a sermon. It is a long one. The sermon is about twenty-five thousand words, which would take four hours to preach nonstop. When you preach your last sermon under circumstances such as those Moses was in, what do you say? What did Moses want the people to remember? Four motifs emerge in Deuteronomy 7:6–11. First, remember that you are a holy people. In the Old Testament, the word *holy* does not mean righteous and moral. It means special to God, different, awe-inspiring. You are a spe-

cial, different, awe-inspiring people, says Moses. It is a
that belongs to Israel and that the church will eventua
"You are a people holy to the LORD your God" (v. 6).

Being holy meant having nothing to do with the ways of the
Canaanites. After all, "The LORD your God has chosen you out
of all the peoples on the face of the earth to be his people, his
treasured possession" (v. 6). The Israelites were like the rooms
in Buckingham Palace that you do not see when you go on the
tour, the rooms that belong especially to the queen. The Israelites
were special to Yahweh. They were to be different. Israel never
took notice of this expectation and instead appointed kings, worshiped by means of images, and traded on the Sabbath like other
peoples. Often Christians do not want to be different either. Forty
years ago Christians were different: We did not go to the pub or
the cinema or go dancing, for instance, and if we did, we knew
we were breaking taboos. Now in many ways we are indistin-
guishable from the world, and it is not obviously a step forward.

So how should we be different? When you think about it, to
call human beings holy is a kind of contradiction in terms. "Holy"
is by definition what makes God God and what distinguishes
God from humans. So what sense does it make to call us holy?

I wonder whether being holy means being supernaturally
human. Holy people are human but in a way that is special, that
is supernatural. The way Ann and I have to be holy is by coping
with Ann's illness. The way anyone else has to be holy will be
different. But as I think of the Christians whom I know best, I
think there is something special, something supernatural about
them in their humanness.

There is a British television program called *How Do They Do
That?* (For instance, how do they make certain tricks work in
television advertisements?) That is what I think of many of my
Christian friends. How does he do that? How does she manage
to be that kind of person? It is probably something they are
unconscious of or take for granted, but for other people it is
what makes them special, what makes them holy. I do not think
much about the heroics of coping with a wife who is disabled,
and I am always a bit astonished when someone else comments
on the patience it requires or on some other aspect of how Ann
and I handle Ann's illness. I know that people find it is something through which God gets access to us in a mysterious way.

And that is true of aspects of who other people are too. As we let the people we are be the people we are with God, the supernatural appears through the human and the world has the opportunity to see that there is something different about us. That is something I would want to leave with people if I were going, like Moses.

But Moses is talking corporately. He is reminding the Israelites that as the people of God they are holy. The same is true of the church. It is always tempting to redefine the church to mean the group we belong to, the bit of the church that we think is alive. It is tempting to be cynical about the church that actually exists, as comes out in our jokes. When Moses says, "You are a holy people," he is talking about the Israel that actually exists. It is the visible church that is holy, and therefore, it is not to be dismissed or despaired of. Remember that you are a holy people.

Second, remember that you are loved. I suggested earlier that it is better, if you have the choice, to fall in love with a friend than to try to make a friend of your lover. Moses implies that this was what God did. He uses two words for love. First, he says, "The LORD did not set his affection on you and choose you because you were more numerous than other peoples" (v. 7). "How did Yahweh come to have those feelings for you, come to be attached to you?" asks Moses. The word for "affection" is one that can describe people's sexual feelings for each other. "Well, it was not because there were so many of you," he answers. This is just as well because Israel's heyday lay in the past.

Perhaps it is the ecclesiological equivalent of, "Will you still need me, will you still feed me, when I am sixty-four? When my hair is gone and I can't stay up as late as I once did, when I've gone pear-shaped and cellulite, will you still love me?" "It was not things about how you looked that made me love you in the first place, silly." "So why did you love me?"

At this point, if you've got Nora Ephron as your scriptwriter, you say as Harry did to Sally in the movie *When Harry Met Sally*, "I love that you get cold when it is 71 degrees out. I love that it takes you an hour and a half to order a sandwich. I love that you get a little crinkle above your nose when you're looking at me as though I'm nuts. I love that when I've been with you all day I can still smell your perfume on my clothes. And I love that you

are the last person I want to talk to before I go to sleep at night."
If you have Hosea as your scriptwriter, it is the same. You say
things like, "When I found Israel, it was like finding grapes in
the desert." But if you are just an ordinary person, you are at a
loss for words and perhaps simply say, "I just did, and I still do."
So it is with Deuteronomy.

Moses moves to the other word for love, the all-purpose
Hebrew word that can mean affection and passion but can also
suggest friendship and commitment. "I did not get attached to
you because there were so many of you. It was just because I
loved you. I found myself committed to you. It had become part
of me. I had to do what I'd told Abraham and Sarah I would do."

Remember you are loved: that God is attached to you and
committed to you, for reasons to do with you maybe, but certainly for reasons to do with God. No matter what seems to happen to the church, God loves it and will continue to be committed to it. God has not finished with it. God will fulfill the
promises made to it.

Third, remember that you are called to knowledge. "Know
therefore that the LORD your God is God" (v. 9), says Moses, and
adds some further theological facts about Yahweh that the people are to know. It sounds like the essence of doing theology,
and it is. But the NRSV rightly translates it as "acknowledging"
these facts about Yahweh, not just knowing them. It assumes
that theology and commitment are one thing, not two things.
That is something Moses wants to leave with the people when
he goes. When theological students are in the classroom, they
are not playing academic games. They are worshiping. And when
they are in chapel, they are not playing religious games. They
are knowing.

What are those facts about God? For Moses, the key one is
that God is faithful and keeps covenant and commitment.

I was glad about that because I felt in special need of it. I left
St. John's because God made it clear that the moment had come.
We were going not so much because God guided as because God
pushed. People would ask me from time to time if I was excited
about it, and the answer was, "Not especially." It was just the
direction God had pushed us. People said we were courageous;
it would have taken more courage for us to stay. But all sorts of
things could have gone wrong. At one point we sent our belong-

ings off though we had not actually completed purchase on the condo we sent them to, nor had we gotten a mortgage. The package with the mortgage information had gone astray in the mail. We had not gotten a visa, and the embassy phone lines were permanently busy. Just before we left we heard that our belongings were not going to arrive before us, as we had planned, and I was not sure how we would work around that. I imagined it would be okay (and it was). There were other more personal things that could have gone wrong, and I had to trust that God is faithful.

Moses offers us various encouragements. He reminds us that Yahweh has been faithful in the past, keeping the promise to Abraham and Sarah. He reminds us that Yahweh exercised divine power and delivered the people. He reminds us that there is a vast disparity between God's responsiveness to lovers and to haters. Punishment for the haters, yes, but faithfulness to a thousand generations for the lovers. One generation will do, thank you. For Ann and me, I was at least encouraged by the signs that it was indeed God who was doing the pushing. If we ended up in a mess and I felt, as I sometimes do, that God could have made my life a bit easier, at least I would know that I was in this hole with God. We have to remember that we are called to knowledge, knowledge of the God who is faithful.

Fourth, remember that you are called to follow God's Word. What Moses says more specifically is, "Take care to follow the commands, decrees and laws I give you today" (v. 11). I do not actually like that. I do not see why God is so keen on giving commandments. I am not very keen on giving commands—why is God? I do not want people to obey me—why does God?

At the moment this is an angle on Scripture with which I am trying to wrestle. Other people will have other questions about Scripture. If there are no aspects of Scripture that you do not like and do not have to wrestle with, then you are kidding yourself. It means you have bracketed them or reinterpreted them.

As a Bible teacher, one of my basic concerns has become simply to get people to read the Bible with open eyes. Some people learn to; others do not. I want people to read the Bible, to be open to finding there things that they had not realized were there, to be enthralled and dazzled and appalled and infuriated and puzzled and worried and stimulated and kept awake at night by these extraordinary words from God, to let their minds and hearts and imaginations and wills be provoked and astonished by them. I want them to follow these words.

If Moses and Israel will commit themselves to that, together and apart, they can cross their river, and he can climb his mountain.

14

Repentance

According to Psalm 32, confession is good for you. You find relief, forgiveness, protection, guidance, and a joy like heaven's own.

As human beings we are all in the condemning and criticizing business (parents-teachers, pastors-congregations, police-community). Perhaps this is partly because inside we feel condemned ourselves. Traditionally, the church has been thought to have a particular preoccupation with sexual sin, despite the wonderful story in John 8 that subverts any such preoccupation. It is a story of a woman who has indeed gone wrong sexually, though we are not in a position to assess degrees of blameworthiness; indeed, to do so would be to subvert the point of the story. The woman is condemned by society, and we assume that God shares the condemning or criticizing attitude.

But we also know that God is not in the condemning business. The cross demonstrates that, but this story shows it too. First, Jesus denies being in the condemning business. Second, he tells the woman she can go, uncondemned. Only after that does he say, "Sin no more." It is easy either to be judgmental or to have no standards. Jesus holds standards and mercy togethe and gets them in the right order. "Neither do I condemn you. . . . Go now and leave your life of sin" (John 8:11). It must be one of the greatest lines in Scripture.

I have the impression that many Christians find sin, guilt, confession, repentance, and forgiveness harder to handle than was once the case. The matter abounds in paradoxes. One is that I notice this condemnatory phenomenon in the evangelical tradition to which I belong, despite the fact that it has always stressed the fact of forgiveness purely on the basis of what Jesus has done for us. Yet this same tradition has also been inclined to a form of legalism, a focus on lists of do's and don'ts. Recently, this has been less so, and we do not feel bound by the taboos of our spiritual forebears (e.g., concerning Sunday observance or alcohol). But we do not seem to be more free, more graceful. Many of us carry around a deep sense of being unworthy, of being stained, of not loving God enough, of not praying enough. It seems that we assume Job's friends are right; our relationship with God depends on what we do, and if we do not do enough, then that relationship is imperiled. We picture God as someone who always has a big stick hidden behind his back, ready to hit us. We often characterize the Pharisees in the Gospels as assuming that they could reach God by doing good; the fact that neither the Gospels nor other sources indicate that this was true of the Pharisees suggests that we may be the perpetrators and victims of the Freudian device of projection, whereby we attribute to other people the characteristics we cannot face in ourselves. Our awareness of guilt is compounded by the more general sense of guilt concerning the way we are spoiling the earth and oppressing the Third World and living off the oppression of the past.

The Harrison Ford courtroom drama *Presumed Innocent* was shown on television last night. It is a story of adultery, murder, guilt, and punishment. Like a good suspense story, it turns the plot upside down during the last ten minutes. Then it actually ends with a soliloquy about punishment—not the punishment the court imposes (for it does not) but the punishment imposed by the guilt with which the protagonists will live for the rest of their lives, knowing what they have done. It is a moral film but a bleak one.

Psalm 130

135

ıs carry around the burden of guilt that the char-
ʾd *Innocent* do, but we have our guilts—not just
true guilts for what we have failed to do. For
ʾides a way to pray and a model of repentant

Repentance involves recognizing the depth of our problem with sin. "Out of the depths I cry to you, O LORD" (v. 1). Praying out of the depths is a common idea in the Psalms. We pray overwhelmed by trouble, overburdened by pressures, pressed down by opposition. In Psalm 130, the problem is not our circumstances or fears or sufferings or doubts but our sins—not what life or other people or God have done to us but what we have done with life and to other people and to God.

Psalm 130 puts an important challenge before us. It asks us whether we see ourselves as sinners, in deep water because of our sin. The psalm implies that we need to be specific about our sin. It speaks not just of sin but of sins such as those of which God might keep a detailed record (v. 3). If we do not see where our areas of sin are, we may need to do some inquiring of God (and some inquiring of other people!).

Repentance involves bowing before the graciousness of a forgiving God (v. 4). Seeing that we are in deep water because of sin can be deeply discouraging. Perhaps our situation suggests that we have a *1984*-kind of God, one who indeed carries a stick behind his back ready to punish us. "Every step you take, every smile you fake, I'll be watching you." "If you, O LORD, kept a record of sins, O LORD, who could stand?" (v. 3).

The words remind us of the tax collector who could not stand before God because he felt he would be shriveled by God's justice, or of Peter shrinking back from Jesus and saying, "Go away from me, Lord; I am a sinful man!" (Luke 5:8), or of another psalm that suggests wherever we go God is able to reach us—we can never get away (see Psalm 139).

But in God's eyes it is not like that. The last word of Psalm 130:2 has already hinted at it. The word is *grace* (though the NIV translates it "mercy"). It is the kind of grace we are familiar with in human experience when someone has every reason to be extremely angry with us and we are amazed to find that he is not. That is how God is. Forgiveness is "with" God (v. 4). It is the very essence of God.

It would be easy to take God's nature for granted and trade on it. Instead, the psalm says, that is why God is feared, held in awe (v. 4). Suppose you let someone down and that person does not hold it against you. If you are really sorry, you do not then trade on that person's forgiveness. You try to do what is best. So it is between us and God. Grace and forgiveness are of the essence of God, and they make us bow before God.

Repentance involves trusting in the word of God (v. 5). In human relationships, we may not know whether we will be forgiven. Nervously, we confess that we have made a mistake, not knowing what the reaction will be. We wait anxiously for the response of the person we have wronged.

The psalm likens our anxiety to someone watching and waiting for the morning (v. 6). Perhaps it refers to the ministers in the temple watching for the dawn and the moment when they are due to offer the morning sacrifice, perhaps to sentries keeping watch in case an enemy attacks. Either way it is a keen-eyed anticipation.

With that keenness we wait for the word of God. Will God forgive? It is his job, Voltaire said. No, says the psalm, you cannot take it for granted. After all, there was more than one occasion in Scripture when a prayer for forgiveness was refused because God knew the people were not really repentant and had not really changed (e.g., Jer. 14:7–10).

But in another sense we can be sure that if we truly turn back to God, God will forgive. The God of Israel is compassionate, gracious, and long-suffering (Exod. 34:6–7). Forgiveness is indeed God's business.

Repentance also involves receiving something that is then our privilege to share (Ps. 130:7). The psalm pictures God giving us both forgiveness and freedom, both mercy and redemption (vv. 7–8). Real repentance does not mean that I stay as I was before. God frees me from sin's penalty and thereby also frees me from sin's power. My problem is that I am in bondage to guilt and self-centeredness, but repentance and forgiveness free me from both of these. That is the psalm's testimony. It speaks of the freedom that comes from being forgiven.

After watching *Presumed Innocent* again, I went to bed awed and grateful that in the real world the Jesus who died and rose is the one who makes it necessary and possible to face guilt but also possible to live with it. That is something to tell the world and the church about.

One October day two years ago, a chaplain at the seminary called to ask whether I would like to join a small group of faculty and chaplains working through the Ignatian Spiritual Exercises. Ignatius of Loyola was a Jesuit priest in the fifteenth century who devised a program of Bible study and meditation to encourage spiritual growth. It has traditionally been used on retreats, but it has been adapted for use on a daily basis over the best part of a year, from fall and Advent to Easter and Pentecost. We would spend an hour each day on our own in Bible study, meditation, and prayer, and we would meet once a week to discuss what we were learning.

In due course, the scheme follows the shape of Jesus' life, and we walk with him through his birth, growth, ministry, death, and resurrection. But two stages prepare the way for that. The first contains reminders of God's loving concern for us and God's involvement in our lives. The second considers our sin. The consideration of sin leads into the reflection on Jesus' coming—it is its background. But the reminders of God's love and involvement are an even more necessary background to the reflection on our sinfulness. At least, I found this latter reflection extremely painful. It made me newly aware of three areas of sin in my life.

During the "sin" stage, I *hated* doing the Bible study and reflection each morning. But it was important to do it. The Ignatian scheme emphasizes consolation and desolation—the way Scripture leads you into encouraging experiences of God and into discomforting experiences. Obviously, one would prefer the former, but thinking about our sin generates the latter. It was just as well that this experience of desolation was set in the context of reminders of God's love and gracious involvement. Ignatius knew what he was doing.

15

Resurrection

Looking Back to the Beginning

There is a hymn by Brian Wren called "Sing My Song Backwards." The idea of it is that there is a sense in which you always have to understand the gospel story from where it ends. When you hear the account of Jesus being crucified, or undertaking his ministry, or being born, you know that the story ends with him being raised in glory, and that makes a difference in the way you read the story as a whole. That is one level on which the Gospels themselves work. Their accounts of Jesus' life and death are stories of someone who is on the way to being raised in glory.

Luke's Gospel, for instance, starts with an explanation as to why Luke is telling his story: It is the basis of Christian faith; these are the things that have been fulfilled and witnessed to and preached. The opening of Luke's Gospel presupposes that Jesus is risen. Then Luke goes back to the beginning of Jesus' story, and we read it in the light of where it is going. Even when we read the opening account of something that happened fifteen months before Jesus was born, we read about this event in the light of the resurrection of Jesus.

Luke invites us to live this story through the lives of Elizabeth and Zechariah. Imagine yourself as one of these two people.

You live in the time of Herod, the Herod who built the temple and who might seem to be on your side. But he has built shrines to other gods as well as fortresses such as Caesarea, Sebastia, and the Antonia in honor of Roman rulers, Roman oppressors. They are the ones who made him king. He is a foreigner with no right to the throne. He has reason to feel insecure about his position, and he does not hesitate to slaughter anyone who looks like a threat to him—the Hasmonean family, who had a claim to the throne as the successors of the Maccabees, or the baby boys of Bethlehem because one of them is believed to be on the way to the throne of his ancestor David.

You are a man or a woman who lives under that kind of political regime. Imagine living under whatever oppressive regime is making the headlines as you read this, or imagine living in Jerusalem itself today. Imagine the insecurity, the subjection, the constraint, the shame, the disgust, the longing for a better future.

You live in the time of King Herod. You belong to the tribe of Aaron, the tribe of priests. It is a position of which to be proud. But you have not let that go to your head. You are someone who puts God first, someone who lives life before God and walks in God's way. You are distinguished for your position but also distinguished for your personal piety.

But you are also someone with a personal inner grief. You have not been able to have children. You have tried for years, seen doctors, and hoped and prayed, but it has never happened. Now you are in your forties, and it looks as though it will never happen.

Yet you know the stories about Sarah and Abraham, and Manoah and his wife, and Hannah and Elkanah. You have shared those stories with other people in distress like yours, and you have told people that this God is your God. Yet such stories have also sharpened the hurt because they do not seem to apply to you. You know that pain keeps the heart soft, and of course you know that the God of Israel is a great God, that the privilege of serving God is worth everything, that having God means you can live with any pain.

But on the dark days, when people say how privileged you are to belong to the priestly tribe, the tribe of Aaron, inside you are tempted to say, "I'd swap with anybody. I'd swap with a Samaritan, if we could only have a baby." And when you think about the way you seek to live close to God and walk in God's way, on the dark days you wonder whether it is worthwhile at all, whether God is really there.

What kind of day is it today, Zechariah, Elizabeth? Workwise, it is a special day. The priests were divided into worship teams that served for a week and then had twenty-three weeks off, which is better than most church rosters. If you were a priest and it was your week on, you had to draw lots for the best privilege, for the task of being the priest who burnt the incense before the Lord in the temple. It was this person who actually sent the prayers of the people up to God. You made the smoke go up, and you prayed for the people, for God's blessing, peace, grace, and compassion. Then you came out and blessed the people. It was something you got the chance to do once in your life, if you were lucky.

And this is your day, Zechariah. And your day, Elizabeth, because it means a lot for you as well. Maybe you have asked yourself why women cannot take part in the way the men do. But all the same, it is precious to you that Zechariah can participate. In spirit you are with him in the temple. Both of you are concentrating on the relationship between Israel and God and Israel's need of God's grace. At least you are trying to concentrate on that, because you know that this is a day more than any other for forgetting yourself and your personal needs. But this moment when your ministry takes you nearest to God, you cannot help also being more aware than ever of the pain in your heart and more agonized than ever by that puzzle at the center of your relationship with God.

Then something happens to you, Zechariah. It is going to be a long time before he can tell you all about it, Elizabeth, but eventually you will hear it from his lips, and you can imagine every detail of the scene. Somebody else is in the holy place. A figure in white stands by the altar and tells you not to be afraid. God has heard your prayer, the prayer that arises from your own pain. Elizabeth will have a baby, and this baby will be the means of bringing Israel back to God, the means of preparing a people for the Lord. He will be God's answer to your personal prayer and also God's answer to the prayer that arises out of your ministry. Your need and Israel's need, your prayer for yourself and your prayer for God's purpose to be fulfilled will be one when they are answered.

This turns out to be an Easter kind of story. It is a story about people with a deep pain in their hearts because God seems to have let them down—about people with a cross in their hearts. It is a story about an angel appearing and banishing fear and declaring that what seemed impossible and undreamable was about to become fact. It is a story about the reality of new life when there seemed only lifelessness and barrenness. It is a story about people whose personal pain was mixed up with the pain that their ministry had brought them and about both pains being healed by an act of God they hardly dared hope for.

Take yourself out of the story for a moment. Name that pain that lies hidden in you. Bring to mind the deep longing that you hardly dare make a matter of prayer because it is evidently not God's will to do anything about it, and thinking about it makes it worse. It is a deep longing that is best forgotten, and you do forget it, except for those moments in the night when you cannot and you cry out in the dark. Imagine that you are standing before God, praying for your people, but you are aware of your pain. Then God says, "Your prayer has been heard." Imagine the impossible becoming possible.

I hesitated to invite you to do that because of the hurt that is involved. I would not have done so merely on the basis of the story of Elizabeth and Zechariah. But I can do it on the basis of reading the story backward, beginning Luke's Gospel after Easter. The resurrection promises that the hope that came to Elizabeth and Zechariah is not the exception; it is the rule. I do not know how or when, but I know that there will be a fulfillment of the vision in Isaiah 25 of the veil of pain and grief and mourning that lies over us being cast away when the Lord swallows up death forever and wipes away the tears from every face. It is Easter truth. It was too overwhelming a promise for Zechariah to cope with. But we have reason to believe it.

At the end of the story both of you, son and daughter of Aaron, have to go back home and get on with the job of life. You are a bit like the disciples after the resurrection but before receiving the Great Commission. You are not saying anything to anyone yet. You go back to the same place, to the same tasks. But you go with a different hope and with new life budding in the womb. You go singing a song that begins with the resurrection and only goes through crosses afterward.

Looking Back to the Passion

In going through the Ignatian scheme, we are invited to accompany Jesus on the journey that starts after his last meal with his disciples, and I did not want to. I was not clear on the point of it. The implication seemed to be that Jesus needs us to do that, and (apart from the metaphysical question of how we can fulfill that need two thousand years after it happened) this seemed sentimental. Yet he wanted his disciples to accompany him. "Could you not stand with me one hour?" "You are the ones who have accompanied me in my trials." Presumably, he wishes us to associate with him in his ministry. It is not part of the plan that he should be alone. It has always been a ministry he wished to share. The people of God are called to be the servants of God. So I walk the way of the cross because I accept my place in this people. I now have another reason not to want to accompany Jesus on this journey. It is now not sentimental but scary.

In the light of what happens in Gethsemane, it is a good thing that while Jesus gives himself to his friends and gets a lot from his relationship with them, he is not dependent on them. When they withdraw or disappear, such acts do not destroy him. He has strength within himself. He can be dependent yet also independent.

He wants Scripture to be fulfilled. He has a destiny, and there is something God wants to achieve through him. He says, "Take this cup from me," but he is also able to say, "Not my will but yours." He combines being sorrowful and troubled with being committed and forthright. Further, he accepts not being in control. He is about to become the object of other people's control—priests, Judas, soldiers, governor. . . . He can cope with that because he knows that on a broader canvas he is in control—or rather, God is. There is thus a beneficent control around the

maleficent one. Things may get out of control but only on a small
scale. In the wider context, things are in control.

As we move from Gethsemane through the scenes that follow, the camera moves farther away from Jesus and focuses
more on other people—Peter, a servant girl, Caiaphas, Pilate,
Herod. Less and less can we look at Jesus' face or know what
he is thinking. Instead, we look in the faces of Barabbas, the
notorious criminal who gets released against all the odds; Pilate,
who is impressed by Jesus but cannot find a way to release him
or cannot find the courage; the religious leaders, who are jealous of Jesus; the crowd, which lets itself be manipulated; and
Pilate's wife, who is troubled by a dream about him. In the way
the story is told, Jesus disappears. And that corresponds to what
is actually happening to him. He is heaved from one person to
another. He is just a victim. He is out of control. He is simply
being acted on by forces that in one sense are all working in
different directions but in another are all coming together to
the same end.

In the Garden, he could have walked out of the situation, as
he had at Nazareth when the people tried to kill him, and maybe
after his death he can bring himself back to life (so John 2:19
implies). But while he is on the cross, he cannot come down. It
is not only a moral impossibility but also a metaphysical one.
The movie Dogma gets it right. Jesus' true assumption of humanity makes that impossible. The only way he can get off the cross
is if God takes him off. This reveals the other aspect to the leaders' mocking and the barb in their final comment: "He trusts in
God. Let him deliver him now, if he wants to." That leads into
"My God, my God, why have you forsaken me?" Only God can
save him now, and God will not do so.

Understandings of the atonement sometimes infer (partly
from that question) that the cross is a moment when Father
and Son are separated, when God's face is turned away. There
is indeed a sense in which the Father's face is turned away. As
the psalms use that expression, the turning away of God's face
means that God does nothing. Yet at the same time, for this to
be the moment when God is in Christ reconciling the world,
the Father needs to be in association with the Son. The Father
is watching as the Son suffers. The Father thus goes through a
different form of suffering from the Son's but one that is just

as real. This is also the case with our suffering. God chooses
not to act but also chooses not to look away and thus suffers
with us.

For days I found all that impossible to think about in a sustained way each morning. It is because of who we are that God
the Father and God the Son suffered. Then the Ignatian lessons
brought us back to John 13, to John's account of the last meal
they had together. There Jesus says that martyrdom is an expression of love on his part. I was focusing on me and why I could
not let him suffer for me. He invited me to look at it from his
angle. Dying is an expression of love, and I was resisting letting
him act in love for me. Even as he walked to the cross, he knew
that his Father had given everything into his hands. I have to
accept his death because I need cleansing. Related to this is the
fact that his experience of suffering is also the moment when
his Father is glorified and when his Father glorifies him.

After that, on Easter Day, I was *relieved* that Jesus was alive.
I had found the weeks of living with Maundy Thursday/Good
Friday wearing—which is of course pathetic, for living with them
is nothing compared to what he went through. But now I was
relieved it was over. The sense of relief started on Holy Saturday. I was relieved just to rest there in the tomb.

The Ignatian notes encourage us to find joy in the fact that
Jesus is risen, but for the following weeks I struggled to do that.
I assumed the problem was that there was something wrong
with the process. There were not enough readings for each week,
or I was getting tired toward the end of the nine months. I eventually realized this was not the problem. There were more profound things going on. Once more, it was an experience of desolation, one that is illuminating.

I saw this when the ordinariness of the scene in John 21 came
home to me. Okay, Jesus is alive, but he is not physically there,
and the disciples are out doing what they have always done—
fishing. As far as they are concerned, his resurrection has not
really changed anything. But Jesus appears (at first in an unrec-
ognizable form) and changes the situation, and they have break-
fast with him. Then they carry on again as they did before, arguing about each other's destiny.

To the very end, the resurrection stories are non-trium-
phalist and not especially joyful. There are no references to

Jesus' joy. Actually, there are no references to what Jesus feels about being alive. There are three references to the disciples' joy but more references to their fear as well as to their grief and worry and unclarity and questioning. Thus, what is most striking is the fact that Jesus' resurrection does not really seem to change things, or rather, it changes things in a dynamic or occasional way rather than a consistent or level way. Things stay the same, then Jesus appears and intervenes and things change, then things go back to being the same, then Jesus intervenes again. . . .

This corresponds to my own feeling and explains why I have not been able to get into the stories as we have been invited to read them. The stress on entering into Jesus' joy does not correspond to the nature of the stories nor to where I am myself. For these two or three weeks, Ann has been coughing somewhat and seems to have more "stuff" in her bronchus. It seems to be bothering her—she murmurs and groans more. For the past three nights, she has been coughing and spluttering, and I therefore have not been sleeping well. Further, for the past two or three weeks she has been getting very constipated, and we have been involved in a round of experiments with fiber and prune juice and suppositories and enemas and the like. One night I spent the hours from ten to midnight cleaning up after a diarrhea episode. Maybe we will find a way through this, but we have not found it yet. Yet Jesus does intervene, and we solve problems for a while. We drive along the cliff edge, but we do not fall off.

Yesterday and today (after that very disturbed sleep) I awoke with joy and began talking to God about how odd that is. I do have joy in life through this, but it is not unalloyed joy. At the end there will be unalloyed joy, I believe. But life now is more mixed. And the resurrection stories are like that. How great God is to give us these stories as they are. I was tempted to say that I live on Holy Saturday, just glad that Jesus is resting in the tomb and off the cross, but that would be gloomier than things are. Life involves an unremitting sequence of sadnesses and losses, but they are interwoven with appearances of Jesus, who shows up to make a difference.

Looking Forward

It is daybreak in Jerusalem. Women are arriving from the villages around, with their bundles of herbs, eggs, and produce to sell near the city gate. There are also three women leaving Jerusalem. They are women of reserve, dignity, and inner pain, grieving for a man they loved, a dead Messiah. They are still coming to terms with the idea of his death and are going to anoint his body. They are confused, and halfway there they realize they will not be able to get into the tomb because of the boulder in front of it.

It is not Easter Sunday in their lives yet. Spring, when the days get lighter and the trees bud, is a peak time for committing suicide. What the calendar says and what nature says conflict with what is happening inside people; they cannot bear the difference. There was a South American Indian tribe exploited and oppressed by government, business, and industry. At Easter they observed only Holy Week, not Easter Day. It was not real for them.

One Good Friday a Christian woman came to see me because she was being assaulted by her husband. She was trying to make the marriage work in a civilized way and to bring their children up happily, but he would turn on her, although she felt she was trying so hard. "There's no justice," I remember her saying, with a Good Friday anguish. It had not changed much by Easter Day. It can still be Good Friday for us when the calendar says Easter Day. At least we can be with people on their Good Fridays.

Then the two Marys and Salome discover something that suggests that Good Friday has passed. The boulder has been moved. Inside the tomb is a young man in a white suit looking as pleased as punch, brushing specks of rock dust from his sleeves: "How about that then?" He has pushed the stone away, not to let Jesus out, for Jesus left a while ago, but to let people in to see that he has gone, to let witnesses see that the tomb is empty.

"No one has stolen the body," the lad says. "That's where he lay, but he has gotten up and gone back to Galilee. He will see you there." And (whoosh) the young man is gone.

Jesus and his friends were never really at home in Jerusalem. Jesus had work to do there, but now he has done it, and he is back up north. Galilee was where God had first sent Jesus to preach and work signs of God's reign. So that is where he is off to. He will see them there, if they want to join him in his mission.

The women were prepared to face up to the fact that Jesus was dead. They were not hiding from reality like the men. They were prepared to adjust, to begin living in the light of reality and loss, of pain and disappointment. Then they find that he is not in the tomb. The young man says he is alive, and they are invited to go and tell the men to begin hoping again.

"Tell the disciples and Peter." Does Peter still count as a disciple, the man who first fell asleep, then disowned Jesus, then kept well away from the cross? People who have done things that make them wonder whether they still count as disciples are invited to put their own name in the sentence—"Tell the disciples and . . . John (or whoever it is) that I will see them in Galilee."

So the women were thrilled to bits and ran to tell them. Not on your life—at least not in Mark's version of the story. At the beginning they are grieving and hurt, at the end trembling and bewildered, running scared and not telling anyone anything. After all, imagine your business is about to fold. You are just getting used to the idea when someone says there is a miracle solution. Do you believe them, just like that, and rush out to tell the world? Aren't you afraid, half-wishing they had not told you because you don't know where you stand now? You don't know what to believe.

The women's silence cannot be the end of what happened, otherwise we would not know about it. Indeed, Mark's Gospel provides a strange account of Jesus' resurrection. Jesus is not even there. Perhaps that enables us to put ourselves into the story. We live our lives between an empty tomb and a Jesus who is already over the horizon, only a cloud of dust. We do not see Jesus being raised from the dead. We have the evidence. There is no corpse in the tomb. He is gone. But it happened before we got here. We did not see him.

Nor can we see Jesus with us now. We will see him when he appears at the end, but that is in the future. We may miss what he is doing or saying in the present because we are blind to it, like those disciples. Mark says to us, "Open your eyes. Get your walking boots on. Jesus is alive. He is off to work in the world. If you hurry you can catch up with him and join in. The Twelve are disillusioned and demoralized; they may not be there. Nobody will do it unless you and I do."

16

Struggle

"I pray . . . that the eyes of your heart may be enlightened in order that you may know . . . his incomparably great power for us who believe. That power is like the working of his mighty strength, which he exerted in Christ when he raised him from the dead" (Eph. 1:18–20). Jesus' being raised to a transformed life is not merely a fact about him (though it is that). It also shows potential available to us.

At the end of Ephesians that theme comes back. "Finally, be strong in the Lord and in his mighty power" (6:10). The strength that is available to us is the power that raised Jesus from the dead. As bishop and theologian David Jenkins once said in a newspaper article, that is not just the power to resuscitate a bag of bones. It is the power to give Jesus a new kind of life, the life of the new age and the new heavens and the new earth. That power is available to us.

And it needs to be. Because "our struggle is not against flesh and blood, but against the rulers, against the authorities, against the powers of this dark world and against the spiritual forces of evil in the heavenly realms. Therefore put on the full armor of God" (6:12–13).

During a meeting of our fellowship group in the seminary we were praying for each other, and I found myself thinking about the group and realizing that in virtually every one of the members God had been at work in a different way. I knew how God had been at work, and I knew that the work often involved pain. In each case, spiritual progress was being made, but the progress was hard work. Indeed, I saw that what was true of these individuals was true of the student body as a whole. The picture that came into my mind was that of trench warfare. We were an army making progress that year. But every inch had to be fought for, every yard was hard work, every foot was paid for in blood, every centimeter required effort because it was met with resistance. We were advancing, but the battle was like trench warfare.

Certain situations could have made us doubt whether God was really at work. As happens in communities, things threatened to waste unnecessary energy and to lead people to misunderstand each other. Those are the marks of being in a battle with forces that like to discourage and deceive. It is a battle in which we are on the way to the blessing that God promises us, but progress toward that blessing involves struggle. It is not a blessing that is easily reached, as we might suppose during some springlike moments of life with God. It is a blessing reached only through conflict. Because "our struggle is not against flesh and blood, but against the rulers, against the authorities, against the powers of this dark world" (6:12).

The Bible does not go into great detail about the nature of the spiritual forces with which we contend. The writers do not seem to know more than you and I know—that there is more to evil than meets the eye. It is not just the sum of its parts. The way we experience evil makes that clear. The Bible does not tell us much more about it but concentrates on pointing us to the way of victory.

We are involved in a struggle against the ruling forces that are masters in a dark age. The powers of evil specialize in ruling, in exercising authority. As far as we can see from Genesis, there was no authority structure designed for human life in the world except the one contained in God. There was no authority of one human being over another. After sin entered the world, however, people began to exercise domination over each other. Human authority and resistance to human authority both belong to this age, not to the age of creation or the age of new creation. Human authority is being exercised in the realm where the powers of darkness operate.

That applies to the world and to the church. When rectors or bishops give in to the temptation to act in an authoritarian or manipulative way, they act under the influence of the powers of darkness. When church councils or pastors either accept that kind of authority or rebel against it, they are working with the assumption that the church operates as an institution that belongs by its inner nature to this age. They are colluding with the powers of darkness. The same is true in a Christian community such as a seminary in the way principal, faculty, and students operate. We get sucked into a way of working that is the way of the powers of darkness.

But Ephesians tells us about the weapons and protection available to us in this conflict.

> Stand firm then, with the belt of truth buckled around your waist, with the breastplate of righteousness in place, and with your feet fitted with the readiness that comes from the gospel of peace. In addition to all this, take up the shield of faith, with which you can extinguish all the flaming arrows of the evil one. Take the helmet of salvation and the sword of the Spirit, which is the word of God.
>
> 6:14–17

This armor and weaponry involve two components: things that involve action and things we simply receive. The passage talks first about three things that involve us doing something: truth, integrity, and witness. Then it talks about three things we receive: faith, salvation, and the gospel.

The three things that involve our activity come from Isaiah (see 11:5; 59:17; 52:7). Truth is the belt that holds us together. Not *the* truth, which would mean the gospel, but simply truth. It is a phrase that describes the armor the Messiah wears. Our own uprightness is one of the things that holds us together in battle. Integrity as our breastplate protects us back and front. It is a phrase that describes the armor God wears in battle. The third item of equipment is the gospel of peace on our feet. The phrase refers to talk in Isaiah about beautiful feet bringing good news of peace to the exiles. Our activity involves being people of truth, integrity, and encouragement.

When I had that picture of trench warfare, I went to talk with one of my colleagues about how it might apply to the seminary. My colleague's word for those aspects of the soldier's armor that point to our responsibility was *holiness*. "What do you mean?" I asked him. He hesitated for a split second and then said, "Sexual purity. I don't mean I suspect there are things going on that shouldn't be. It's just that I know from my own heart that sexual purity is an area we always have to protect."

It is not merely a question of sex outside marriage being wrong, partly because we who are married can then be let off too lightly. Selfish sex within marriage is also sinful. Perhaps one of the key questions that a person has to ask about a relationship is how far it is actually selfish, how far I am in it for the other person's benefit. That is surely one of the key moral questions about sexual relations. It is not merely a question of what you do with certain parts of your body. It concerns the fairness of what you are doing, why you are doing it, what in the end this activity and this relationship will do to the other person and to other people to whom you have commitments. Those questions are raised sharply by every act of extramarital sex, but they are also raised uncomfortably by every act of marital sex. Is it really an act of love? It is interesting that God's words to Eve in Genesis 3 put together authoritarianism and sexual selfishness as the consequences of humanity's disobedience: "Your desire will be for your husband, and he will rule over you" (v. 16). To love and to cherish becomes to desire and to dominate (so says Derek Kidner in his commentary on Genesis).[1]

Sexual relationships have become for our age a key means by which you realize yourself, and Christians are inevitably affected by that sort of expectation. It is interesting that in the preceding chapter of Ephesians the question of the significance of sex was raised in quite different terms. There we get explicit instruction on the significance of sex, with the only explicit biblical teaching on the headship of a man over his wife. The passage makes it absolutely clear that a biblical doctrine of headship exists, and it makes it clear what that doctrine is. Men have the

unquestionable right and responsibility to let themselves be crucified for women, and women must submit to them in the sense
of letting them do that.

It is typical that Scripture should take a worldly assumption
and let the cross turn it upside down. The world says, "Men have
authority over women." The Bible says, "Yes, they have the
authority Christ showed on the cross." Biblical headship is not
about men deciding how to bring up the children or where the
family should live. It is about letting yourself be walked on. That
is the Bible's pattern for relations between the sexes. Marriage
gives you many chances to live that way; single people are called
to make that their criterion for their relationships too. In our
relationships, the other person comes first.

Truth, integrity, and encouragement are responsibilities we
exercise, important ones if we are to be protected in our conflict. Let them be the way we relate to one another as sexual
beings. There will be other areas of holiness we have to think
about, of course, and we will also need to think out what truth,
integrity, and encouragement mean in relation to them.

Then there are the shield, which is faith, and the helmet,
which is salvation, and the Spirit's sword, which is the word
God speaks. They are things you receive. So here in Ephesians
the challenge comes first, and the grace you need to meet the
challenge comes second. We certainly need the gospel at this
point, because we all fail as sexual beings, just as we fail in the
way we cope with exercising authority or reacting to it, and in
other areas. We can be driven into more failure precisely by the
awareness of failure and guilt. We need armor to protect us from
that.

It is not just the feeling of guilt, which as people of our particular era we may be inclined to concentrate on, but the fact of
guilt. We carry such knowledge around with us: the things we
know we have done, the things we wish we had done. They
become unbearable burdens that drive us into more failure,
unless the gospel is applied to them. Ephesians reassures us that
faith quenches all the fiery darts of the evil one. The evil one
throws our failures into our face, loves to make us feel more and
more guilty and paralyzed and driven to despair and to more
failure. Faith is a shield that stops those burning arrows because
it is faith in Christ as our Savior.

There is not a lot of difference between the pieces of armor. Suppose the evil one rubs my nose in the fact that I am a sexual failure—not in the sense that the world thinks of sexual failure; in those terms, I might be a sexual success. But in terms of expressing integrity, uprightness, and encouragement in my relationships I might be a failure. At that point Jesus utters those wonderful words in John's Gospel: "I do not condemn you." Those are the kinds of words about salvation that my faith clings to and that serve as a sword to fight off the evil one's attack.

There is one more thing this passage in Ephesians presses on us. "Constantly ask God's help in prayer, and pray always in the power of the Spirit. To this end keep watch and persevere, always interceding for all God's people. Pray also for me" (6:18–19). Prayer is a subject that can often make people feel guilty rather than free. These words in Ephesians are an exhortation: They are about the responsibility of prayer, but they are not designed to make us feel guilty. Rather, they remind us of another resource we have in the spiritual battle we wage together.

"Pray at all times in the Spirit, with all prayer and supplication. . . . Keep alert with all perseverance, making supplication for all the saints," the RSV puts it more literally. In his commentary on Ephesians, John Stott points out that this passage does not say "sometimes with some prayer and some perseverance for some of your brothers and sisters" but all prayer and all perseverance for all the saints at all times.[2] Perhaps Christians might think about covenanting to pray for each other in that way as they engage in trench warfare with the evil one. It sounds like another key to the battle for the blessing being won.

"Keep watch," we are told. "Be alert." Take Jesus as your model for the way you operate by resurrection power. The power that brought Jesus back from the dead is available to us, and it needs to be if we are to reach the blessing God has promised us. It is not just the power to resuscitate a bag of bones; it is the power that gave Jesus a new kind of life—the life of the new age and the new heavens and the new earth. It is available to us.

17

Tears

I cannot remember whether I used to cry fifteen years ago. I do not think I was especially averse to crying or was embarrassed by the idea or felt that I had to keep a stiff upper lip in all circumstances. I do not remember it being an issue. But I am aware that in recent years I have found myself crying relatively often.

Like many people, I cry at movies. I wept near the end of *Once upon a Time in America* and *Paris, Texas* and *When Harry Met Sally* and *The English Patient* and *Leaving Las Vegas*. I am sure there are others, but those are among my favorite films. I wept at the beginning of *Sleepless in Seattle* and again at the end. It was the only time I wept at both ends of a film. All those films contained something about the toughness of human experience, about pain or loss, about guilt or helplessness, about bondage to our personalities or our past, about bravery or acceptance of the inevitable, or about happiness that you did not believe would ever come (even if you knew the plot required it).

I also sometimes want to cry during my own sermons, and essentially for the same sort of reasons. I used to preach a sermon on Samson (before it appeared in print in *After Eating the*

Apricot), and I always had to hold back a tear at the last line of it, at the fact that Samson, who fell so far short of all he should have been, is in the cloud of witnesses in Hebrews 11. If there is room for Samson, there is room for you and me. And in this book I have referred to a number of occasions when I have found myself in tears. I have wept because I was afraid I could not sustain the demands that my job placed on me. I have wept at the reminder of the commitment I made to let God be my only desire. I have wept when talking students through the story of Job. I have wept when becoming overwhelmingly aware of God's love. I have wept when saying good-bye to people, at losing people. I have wept when recognizing my loneliness and the length of the journey and the number of rivers there are to cross. I have wept when having to take Ann for a routine stay at her rehabilitation center. I have wept at the awareness of God's rejoicing in me. I have thus wept at sad moments and more strikingly at moments of joy. I have found that weeping and discovering what our tears mean may be part of acknowledging hurts and sins from which we have hidden and may thus be part of finding forgiveness and healing.

Tears are strange things. Maggie Ross has written a book about tears called *The Fountain and the Furnace: The Way of Tears and of Fire.* She talks about the connection between the gift of tears and the gift of joy and about the way tears unlock joy. They can signify that we are giving up self and thus finding self; so in death is life. The salt of tears is the savour of life.[1] Tears, she says, are a mark of having touched reality.[2] I have mentioned John of the Cross, who talks much (as other mystical writers do) about our love relationship with Jesus. He often refers to Scripture in this connection, especially to the Song of Songs. The trouble is that the Song of Songs seems to have been a collection of ordinary human love songs, not poems about our love for God. That awareness about the original meaning of John's favorite book sent me off on a hunt for passages of Scripture that directly refer to an emotional love relationship between us and God. These turned out to be difficult to find. I was then interested to discover that the person who most clearly reveals an emotional love for Jesus does so with tears (Luke 7:38).

I can think of four possible reasons for my own greater susceptibility to tears. The first is that I have grown older. One of the things that happens, people say, as you reach middle age, is that sides of your personality that you had not previously realized can find expression—you can own your "shadow side." For me, tears may be part of the complement to a hardness with both positive and negative sides that was more characteristic of me for my first forty-odd years. The second is that because of Ann's illness I have felt more pain over the past fifteen years than in earlier years of my life. The third is related to the first two. The tears issue from having God pierce a way into my life through the fact that Ann and I have had to live with Ann's illness. That has perhaps reached into me and brought to the surface realities and capacities that would otherwise have lain unrealized.

The fourth is quite unrelated, except in the providence of God. The tears are linked in some way to my position as a seminary principal. I felt some ambiguity about becoming a principal. I used to say that I had no desire or need to be in charge of the seminary, to be the number one, to carry that responsibility. I deserve to have had someone say that I behaved as if I were in charge of the place even when I was not, and in that sense, I had no need to be formally in charge. I had the advantages of being involved in leadership without the disadvantage of formal responsibility. It was certainly the case that one of the great things about the seminary, which I remember discovering in my first faculty meeting, was that if you had a good idea, it would be recognized and accepted even if you were the most junior person in the place. Conversely, if you could not get people to recognize the strength of your idea, mere seniority in the system would not enable you to get it implemented.

On the other hand, I may secretly have suspected that as principal I would have the opportunity to exercise different forms of influence. I could shape agendas and set styles and throw my weight about. Once in a meeting when we were discussing a proposal, I said very firmly something like, "I cannot agree to that," and we decided not to do it. Later over tea there was an interesting discussion about (1) whether I was vetoing the proposal, (2) whether people let it fall because they thought I was vetoing it, or (3) whether people let it fall because I felt so strongly about it. I did not know what I was doing, though if challenged I think I would have seen the remark as a contribution to debate not an end to debate, and I would have recognized (indeed, in the discussion I pointed out) that I had no power to veto things. But subconsciously I may have intended the ambiguity and may have intended to short-circuit the debate. Becoming principal meant that my relationship with power became more ambiguous than it had been previously.

I knew there was some link between tears and that feeling of ambiguity about power, though I was not sure what the link was. It was about then that I became acquainted with the writings of Maggie Ross. In her later book, *Pillars of Flame: Power, Priesthood, and Spiritual Maturity,* she takes up the conviction that priesthood ought to reflect God and who God is in Christ.

> What God does is God's priesthood reaching across the abyss of illusion we create by presumption to control. As God's image we seek to mirror God's outpouring. God creates with self-abnegation outpoured, continues and sustains this creation *by going to the heart of pain that dwells within the Creator's self-restraint and is inherent in creation's freedom, and from this total self-denudation God generates new life, hope, and joy.*[3]

Tears are central to emptying oneself of one's glory; they "are a sign that we are struggling with power of one sort or another: the loss of ours; the entering of God's."[4] More generally:

> If we are to mirror God, to be in God's image . . . we have to be willing to enter our individual wounds and through them the wounds of the community. . . . We have to be willing to enter the wound of God. We have to be willing to enter these wounds, not hide them by casuistry, not seal them up, nor scar them over.[5]

We can attempt to avoid this by seeking pseudo-healing that removes from us the possibility of the resurrection that comes through "learning to live with, in, and through pain, to adjust to our wounding."[6]

In recent years, there has been some talk of "the gift of tears." That talk invites us to see tears as inspired by the Spirit in a way that perhaps parallels tongues—each is both wordless and expressive. Tears are a gift that may make us able to empathize with others, to express our prayer for them in a physical way, to free them to express their own hurt or joy, and to free ourselves to express ours. What my own experience reflects is that if there is anything spiritual about tears, they have the same mixture of supernatural and natural as other gifts do (not least tongues).

In addition to Isaac the Syrian, to whom Maggie Ross refers, one of the classic writers on tears is Teresa of Avila, a sixteenth-century Spanish spiritual writer. In *The Interior Castle,* one of the great classics on the development of our relationship with God, she notes that tears can be of supernatural or natural significance.

> I have seen people shed tears over some great [natural] joy; sometimes, in fact, I have done it myself. It seems to me that the feelings which come to us from Divine things are as purely natural as these, except that their source is nobler. . . . Worldly joys have their source in our own nature and end in God, whereas spiritual consolations have their source in God, but we experience them in a natural way. . . .
>
> If I began to weep over the Passion, I could not stop until I had a splitting headache; and the same thing happened when I wept for my sins. This was a great grace granted to me by Our Lord, and I will not for a moment examine each of these two favours and decide which is the better. . . . The tears and longings sometimes arise partly from our nature and from the state of preparedness we are in; but nevertheless . . . they eventually lead one to God.
>
> Note also that distress of this kind is apt to be caused by weak health, especially in emotional people, who weep for the slightest thing; again and again they will think they are weeping for reasons which have to do with God but this will not be so in reality.
>
> Do not let us suppose that if we weep a great deal we have done everything that matters. . . . Let the tears come when God is pleased to send them: we ourselves should make no efforts to induce them. They will leave this dry ground of ours well watered and will be of great help in producing fruit; but the less notice we take of them, the more they will do.[7]

Tears can be something that God sends or that God uses, or they can have purely human significance. Many people use up three tissues in a film, under cover of darkness. Mothers are able to determine if tears are merely an attempt at manipulation, and God is not won over by the mere sight of tears (Mal. 2:13; Heb.

12:17). They need to be an indication that something profound is going on. They need to be an expression of true grief and not mere remorse, of true love and not mere self-love.

In Scripture and in Christian history, tears have been a natural part of praying for other people and of praying for oneself. They vividly express the complex interweaving of body, spirit, feelings, mind, and subconscious. Sometimes we may be aware that all five are working together. Sometimes tears well up for reasons that the mind may not yet know.

In the prayers in Psalms, people use all sorts of devices to gain God's attention, to get God to take note of their pain and hurt. Drawing attention to their tears is one such device. "All night long I flood my bed with weeping and drench my couch with tears" (Ps. 6:6). "My tears have been my food day and night" (Ps. 42:3). If we are hurt, the Psalms assume, the natural thing is to cry; and if we are hurt before God, we cry before God and expect God to notice, as a child cries before his or her mother and expects her to notice (cf. Ps. 39:12; 56:8). Crying is one of the things we need to learn from children.

On one occasion I found myself weeping for a student who had a particular pain in his life. There was probably a selfish element to those tears. I saw my own loss mirrored in his. I was weeping for myself as well as for him. But I *was* weeping for him, and my feeling of grief meant I was putting myself in his place and weeping with one who was weeping. When that happens to us, we are involved in intercession. As the Bible sees it, intercession involves standing in someone else's place and speaking for that person, speaking as that person, identifying with that person. If I weep for someone, I can ask God to preserve those tears too, to note those tears, even as I may ask God to note mine, to preserve mine, to be motivated by mine.

Jeremiah was once referred to as the "weeping prophet." He wanted his tears to overflow for his people because of the loss their sin had put them through and because this sin threatened to put them through more loss (see Jer. 9:1; 14:17). His tears accompanied his pleas for God not to cast the people off, not to act as if despising them, not to keep afflicting them like the oppressors who cause people to weep without self-consciousness or calculation because of their oppression (Eccles. 4:1), not to abandon the covenant relationship with the people (Jer. 14:19–21).

Jeremiah also shed tears on the people's behalf as he confessed their sin, which is needed if God is to heed that prayer (14:20). Those tears were shed in their stead. He shed other tears because of his own grief at that sin and his awareness of where it would lead (13:17). Paul similarly wept over the enemies of the cross of Christ (Phil. 3:18). When Jesus wept over the city of Jerusalem, he took up Jeremiah's ministry (Luke 19:41–44).

Just as we cannot experience the joy of answered prayer without offering prayers, so we cannot experience the joy of having our tears wiped away without having shed some (cf. Luke 6:21). That applies both to tears on our own behalf and to tears we weep for others. But if we have shed tears, then we can prove that those who sow in tears (not believing that there can ever be a harvest again, that the laughter of the past can ever be laughter in the present) do reap in joy (Psalm 126). And we can know that the disaster that causes tears is not God's last word (see Isa. 25:8; taken up in Rev. 7:17; 21:4).

Jesus' ministry shows that this wiping away of tears is not an experience for which we necessarily have to wait until the end. He acts on behalf of the weeping widow at Nain, and therefore, she can stop weeping (Luke 7:13). At Bethany he does not merely tell people they have no need to weep; he first allows himself to be drawn into their weeping (John 11:31–35). He asks Mary Magdalene why she is weeping and in addressing her by name wipes away her tears (John 20:11–16).

18

Trust

Moving to California involved me in my first serious exercise in trust in thirty years. I felt as if I were walking a plank or a tightrope with deep water below.

Mark Knopfler's song "Love over Gold" was already one of my three all-time favorite songs, but I came to feel that it described not only the person I wished I was but also the person I had been forced to become. The song is addressed to someone who walks out on the high wire and dances on thin ice without paying heed to the danger or to people's advice. She (I presume) goes dancing through doorways just to see what she will find and embodies the need to value "love over gold," throw caution to the wind, and take the risk of sharing love with strangers. One should not be held back by the possibility that "the things that you hold can fall and be shattered, or run through your fingers like dust."

A year before, I had received a phone call from the dean of the School of Theology at Fuller Theological Seminary in Pasadena, near Los Angeles. We had met four years earlier in South Africa, and we had talked about the possibility of my visiting there one day to teach a course or two. This can be a way of testing out whether a school might like to offer a post to someone, and I knew the school had an Old Testament position to fill.

I had been principal of St. John's Theological College, Nottingham, for nearly nine years, and at that stage, I think I had begun to solidify the notion that ten years would probably be enough. At St. John's we were involved in a major development project, and that time frame seemed likely to see the process well under way, which would make the ten-year mark a feasible time for a change. In the New Year, I was still feeling settled enough to buy a new VCR and join a book club, yet I began to feel more rather than less unsettled. It began to seem that there were ways in which it would be good to have a change of principal sooner rather than later. The college was developing in interesting ways, but it was also facing some pressing challenges, and I believed it needed a differently shaped person at the helm. This meshed with my own feeling of tiredness with the responsibility of being principal. I had felt that tiredness before but had sensed that God was telling me to gird up my loins and was promising to be my strength. This time, however, I felt that God was giving me permission to give up.

A few weeks later I heard a sermon from a bishop on the importance of not giving up, and I might have expected to be thrown by that, but instead I found myself saying, "Yes, that's true in principle, but I know that God is saying something different to me at this moment."

One evening I expressed the unsettledness to a friend, which helped to make me feel settled about feeling unsettled and thus able to regain peace and joy in Christ. I began to consider visiting Fuller after Easter so that if the school offered me a job and we liked it there, I might agree to go and thus resign my post at St. John's. But over the next weekend I realized that I wanted to dissociate the two questions. Whether it was time to leave St. John's and where we should go were two separate questions. From St. John's angle, if I resigned early in the year rather than waiting until after Easter, the school could appoint my successor, with the prospect of a straight handover in the summer. From my angle, there simply were two questions, and once I had gotten clear on one, it seemed strange to make it depend on the other.

The day I was writing to the trustees and the faculty to tell them that I intended to resign, a student wrote to me to say the things about community that I quoted in chapter 4. I told another of our friends, who said that for a while she too had been feeling led to pray for us without knowing why. I told one of Ann's companions, who said that her husband had been sensing a special impetus to pray for us without knowing why. I took these as signs that we had been surrounded by God's protection during the preceding weeks and that the decision to go was right (which another friend pointed out to me was an important conviction given the possibility that things could go wrong!).

A week later I was to tell the student body that I was resigning, and I was feeling odd and behaving oddly. I was responding in illogical ways to things that happened or to things that people said, the way you do (or I do) when you are under stress or worried. I had to drive up the freeway to speak at a meeting, and once again this gave me the opportunity for a long conversation with God in which I could work out what was going on. I realized that four feelings were finding expression in my odd behavior. I felt a failure for not being the kind of principal the seminary needed. I felt guilty for causing Ann to move when she would rather stay. I felt an anticipatory bereavement at the loss of people I love and who love me. And I was afraid of not finding others and of being alone. Being able to identify and name these feelings solved much of the problem, not least because I could argue with myself about them in the way Psalms 42 and 43 urge. You cannot argue until you have named. At the same time, they remained the areas for which I had to trust God as the move drew near.

Although the telephone call from Fuller played a key part in my decision to resign, I could not assume that the job there was a certainty. Fuller was considering two or three other people for the post. I did not know how the American medical insurance system worked and was not sure whether it would be financially feasible for us to abandon the arms of the British National Health Service and the social services. Neither Fuller nor I could know if we were meant for each other until we had met properly. So I needed to treat a move there as one possibility; it was no foregone conclusion.

When I resigned without knowing what I would do, I met reactions I was not prepared for. The seminary seemed almost hurt, as well as stunned and threatened. Students at a seminary tend to exaggerate the extent to which the principal influences the seminary. Yet I remember that when I was being interviewed for the position I said I saw the post in terms of a guardianship of the college's relationship with God or of its spirituality. If a person who has sought to focus on that goes, then that makes a difference.

One bishop said to me, "In the Church of England, you just do not resign one job until you have the next" and referred to Abraham's going out not knowing whither he went. Indeed, one of my colleagues had done that a year previously, resigning his post because he thought the time had come and because he thought he was about to be offered another; it gave me pause for thought that his possibility then fell through, though something else fine emerged. "Are you really jumping off the cliff without a safety net?" my rector asked, to which the answer was, "Well, we could live with my mother, and I could become a freelance theologian." (I had not asked my mother, though when I mentioned the possibility, she did start mentally reorganizing her house.) Or I might be able to become a part-time rector and freelance theologian, and that might even enable me to be a part-time Old Testament lecturer in a seminary that might need one. Because there were such safety nets, I did not exactly feel that I was jumping off a cliff.

Soon there followed our college Quiet Day. A guest speaker gives two or three talks, and then there is space in the rest of the day for people to do dealings with God. I had normally gone to the talks, but I confess that I had usually let the rest pass me by. This time, however, it seemed appropriate not to do so. The speaker encouraged us to write a letter to God, and this is what I wrote.

> I like the idea of writing to you, Father—it fulfills the function of getting it out of my head, but doing it in conversation with you, and you can comment.

I am excited about the possibility of going to Fuller. You know that last Tuesday we had that lovely evening with three people from Fuller who enabled us to have a much clearer picture of what it would be like, and that on Friday I had that amazing e-mail from the dean giving me encouraging responses to all my questions. It looks as if health care and housing and caretakers for Ann will not be a problem, and the job description places such an emphasis on research and writing. And I remembered that when I was articulating what I thought you were giving me permission for, in saying it was okay to leave here, I was instinctively putting it in terms of being free to be a "writer, priest/pastor, and teacher," and I thought the order must be wrong—an institution would be concerned if it thought I was mainly interested in writing. But this does not seem to be so!

The instinct to put "priest/pastor" second is interesting, and I commit myself to that order if the job does come off. Maybe that will help with the loneliness question, which is now the chief thing I am a bit anxious about. I am visualizing it as a bit like North Park [a seminary in Chicago that I had visited a little while before], with the seminary occupying the kind of space in Pasadena that North Park did there, near restaurants and shops interwoven. It will be really nice if we can find a house within a few minutes of that (like the ones in North Park) so that I can push Ann there. I think you are encouraging me to hope.

The e-mail made me feel a bit as if it was not only too good to be true, but too good to be right. I also remembered a sense that you were saying that enough was enough, that I had worked hard over the past decade with Ann and with St. John's, and that you wanted me now to have an easier time and do what I wanted.

The letter we were invited to write also involved giving to God people (whom I was concerned about, whom we would miss), situations (such as the future of St. John's), weaknesses and temptations (such as needs I was aware of and the possibility that we would either have not enough money or too much), and hopes (that the post at Fuller would work out, that there would be happiness in the future for me and for Ann). I had not had the faith to ask God to make Ann happy about going to America, but before we went for our visit, she was talking as if she wanted to—or was at least saying it was exciting even if she would really prefer to stay in England.

We flew to Los Angeles on Tuesday, April 1. During our first night, I was wide awake at 1:00 A.M. (it was 9:00 A.M. by my body clock). I got up and started to read the tourist information on Los Angeles that the seminary had kindly left for us and found myself instantly disenchanted with the prospect of living near Hollywood, Beverly Hills, and Venice Beach. (I eventually realized that Pasadena is a self-contained community with its own shops, cinemas, theaters, and music, so if you want to stay away from L.A., you can do so.) I wondered why we were there at all and how we could get out of the situation.

Yet what emerged over the next few days was that the job was right for me and that God had checked things out ahead of us. If there was any school where I could be a writer, pastor, and teacher, this was it. I had feared that the theological atmosphere would be less congenial than at St. John's, but I felt very much at home. The people were lovely, even if I allowed for the possibility that (as someone put it) Americans are better at being friendly than at being friends. I could see some of them falling in love with Ann, as people do.

On Friday the realtor took us to some possible houses. She showed us three or four single-story houses, which was what I had said we wanted, but my heart sank as I entered each one. I could not see us in any of them. They had tricky doorways and turns that would be difficult for Ann and the wheelchair to negotiate, and they looked high-maintenance.

Then she took us to a three-story condominium. I do not know why she did that, because we had said we wanted a house. But as we walked through the lobby with its sitting area, cool and open to the sky, I felt at home and could see us there. It was easy to push the wheelchair around the ground-floor open-plan condo. There was a study area separate from the living room, a version of the way we had arranged things at our home in Nottingham so that I can be with Ann but still working.

In due course, we walked into the bathroom and saw a walk-in shower of the kind we had installed in our home in Nottingham. I half saw the hand of God pointing and half heard God saying, "Do you see?" which I took to mean, "I've been here before. I knew this was here. It's for you." I say "half saw" and "half heard" because at the time it seemed naive and too risky even to think that that might be what was going on. But as weeks

ned confidence in believing that this was for us. It
ificant that the seller was an Episcopalian who was
lling to someone in Christian ministry and was will-
the price by $15,000. It seemed significant that the
d on the market until I was offered a job and accepted it; subsequently, another sold at a higher price within
five days.

Ann coped well with the journey and if anything moved a little easier than she had been doing in Britain. This confirmed
the possibility that the climate would be good for her. The dean,
whose sister-in-law has multiple sclerosis, pointed out that California has a desert climate—sunny and hot but with low humidity. Trips to the Alps had showed us that the combination of
warmth and low humidity suited Ann.

One Wednesday, nearly three weeks after we had returned to
Britain, we had a time of seeking God in chapel, and God told
one of our students, "Tell John, 'Judges 18:6.'" "I don't know
what it says," she replied, "and I haven't got a Bible." "Never
mind," said God, "just tell him, 'Judges 18:6.'" Later in the cor-
ridor she pressed into my hand a scrap of paper bearing this reference and told me what had happened. "Judges 18? That's the
story of the Levite's concubine being cut into twelve pieces, isn't
it?" I said. "I hope not," she replied (actually, that is Judges 19,
though as a whole Judges 18 is fairly tough stuff too). We both
went home to look it up. In the NIV, it reads, "Go in peace. Your
journey has the LORD's approval." The NRSV says, "Go in peace.
The mission you are on is under the eye of the LORD." I checked
the Hebrew, which says more literally, "Go in peace. The road
on which you are going is before Yahweh." The word for "before"
is a rare one. The dictionary explains that in contexts such as
this it means "under Yahweh's eye and favorable regard."

The next day I received an email offering me the job at Fuller.
I printed out the message, wandered about with it that day, and
slept on it, though I knew there was only one response I could
make. The next day I went to the computer again and typed a
short note of acceptance. As I paused before I pressed the "send"
key, intending perhaps to think and pray one more time, a colleague came in to ask me about something. We had a brief conversation, and I turned back to the keyboard. I found that actu-

ally I had pressed the "send" key. It was too late for further thoughts. That somehow seemed right and typical.

The readings and prayers that Sunday were just for me. We prayed to God who can bring order to our unruly wills and passions. We heard God promising to turn desolation into beauty. We heard God knocking at the door, seeking to be let in. We heard God asking, "Do you love me more than these?"

Over the next few weeks, some funny things happened. For a while it seemed that we were caught in a kind of catch-22. Our mortgage broker wanted us to sign documents at the U.S. embassy in London during June. Our immigration attorney wanted us to do nothing about the loan until we had visas. If we waited for visas, it would be too late for the loan. Or we could lose both the loan and the visas. . . . In due course, the two situations became unlinked and the house purchase was going through. I wired our payment to the agent. The money failed to arrive. The Fuller bursar asked for reference numbers to trace the transaction. By the time I had the reference numbers, it was Independence Day, and everyone had left for a long weekend. After the weekend the money reappeared from cyberspace, the sale went through, and we were owners of a condominium in California.

Of course, there was a chance we might not get visas; we would own property in the United States but would be unable to enter the country to earn the money to pay for it. Indeed, the embassy initially refused our visa application; Ann's photograph was too small. Fortunately, that was their biggest problem with us, and we eventually received the visas. Then I really believed we were going.

From time to time I fretted about Ann. We had warm spring weather in April, and our garden looked lovely; I could not imagine her enjoying looking out on our patio in Pasadena in the same way. I had to give that to God, believing the signs of God's involvement. From time to time I was overwhelmed by the stress of all the questions involved in the move. What if we did not find the caregivers we needed to look after Ann? What might issue from the fact that we did not really know how the medical system works in the United States and what it will deliver? What if I am unable to cope physically? What if I am unable to cope emotionally? I was to have that recurrent feeling that I had never been so pushed out in faith, having to trust in demanding circumstances.

By then the stakes had been raised. During the summer term, Ann had been getting less mobile and in late June had a relapse of her illness. She could no longer stand at all, and her urinary catheter system no longer worked. She was admitted to her rehabilitation center for four weeks and came out less mobile than she had been when she went in. This markedly changed the nature of the task of caring for her. I learned to use a patient lift, but the medics were uncertain about how to handle the catheter problem. I realized neither Fuller nor I had a bottomless purse to cover possible nursing costs. All this heightened the pressure of the fact that we were moving away from the people who love us and whom we love.

So what does trust mean? What can I trust God for? There had been all those signs that God was taking us from the UK to the USA, and in a dream I could imagine that everything would be wonderful. We would get the caregivers. We would get the health care. Ann's catheter system would work, or we would find some other arrangement. I would be able to walk her into the town for a film or ice cream or shopping. We would attract squirrels and birds onto our patio. But I was making the mistake of trying to imagine a neat future by analogy with the present, the way you have to when you think of heaven. I had to remind myself that in a new situation, things working out well and in a way that made Ann happy would be different and perhaps unimaginable.

There was a much tougher fact that I had to remind myself of. There were all those signs that God was taking us from the UK to the USA, yet I was hesitant to believe that God was promising us a rose garden, that the signs implied that everything was bound to go well. Somehow things do not necessarily work out that way. After all, we had sought God's will concerning marriage, but that had not stopped it from being tough.

So what is one entitled to expect? What does God's faithfulness consist of? My own experience has been that each extra bit of pressure has been but the harbinger of another one. God treats me rather the way a trainer treats a weightlifter. The satisfaction you get is not that of being able to give up lifting weights. Succeeding at one weight simply qualifies you to try the next. When the possibility of going to Pasadena first arose, it felt like a gift, like the trainer's permission to rest. By the time we were about to leave, it felt more like the context in which to lift more weights. The faithfulness of God consists of not requiring you to lift what will break your back; the promise is that God does not let us be tested beyond our strength. I trust that in personal ways things will not be overwhelming, that I will be able to carry the inner burden, and that in financial ways things will not be overwhelming.

After I had been away for a day, on getting back to Nottingham I went to see Ann in the rehabilitation center. She was in bed, and she greeted me with a surprised smile. I had written on her message board that I would be there late and had asked the nurses to remind her; perhaps they had done so and she had forgotten. She had had no visitors. I had asked God to send someone, but there had apparently been no one. Her contentedness seemed to make that unimportant. On my way out a nurse stopped me to ask one or two things and then talked about how wonderful it was that we were going to America and how wonderful Ann was. She told me how much they had been laughing in the afternoon as they had been getting her to bed with the lift and how wonderful her sense of humor was. I went home crying but content, as I often am, feeling that for me and for Ann God had not done what I had asked but had ministered to me and to her in ways that made that okay.

Two weeks later, Ann came home. For twenty-four hours it seemed that looking after her was all there was time to do. I got up with a sense of hopelessness the next day. In the mail I found a bon voyage card from a former student. It was embroidered on the front with a boat bearing the stars and stripes and our initials, and superimposed on this was the cross. Inside it talked about what St. John's had meant to this person and the blessings that had come through Ann's illness. The previous day I had been reading 2 Corinthians 4 because I had to preach on it a week or two later: "Death is at work in us, but life is at work in you" (v. 12). That has been Ann's story. And mine, in a way.

That night I had a dream. Near our home is a six-lane street with a complicated junction. At the time the road was being repaired, and only four of the six lanes were open. As you drove along you switched from one lane to another, sometimes with holes and barriers on one side, sometimes on the other. In my dream, the junction itself was under reconstruction, and I was traveling through it on a bus. There was only the narrowest of paths through the roadworks, and the surface was not tarred. Indeed, the road was not actually wide enough for the bus, and it crumbled down on either side into deep gulfs. But the bus made its way briskly and confidently through the junction and on toward our home. I took that as God's promise regarding the journey we were about to undertake. Later I discovered that when God promises to make the way of the righteous smooth (in Isaiah 29), the word for "way" is the word for a cart-track, and cart-tracks are pretty uneven.

Soon every day contained good-byes, each of which took a little part of us. On our farewell Sunday at our church, one of our churchwardens gave us a card with the promise, "God is not a deceiver that he should offer to support us and then when we lean upon him should slip away from us."

Before we left, I felt that God's own trustworthiness was on the line and it was so because God had put it there. If things went wrong, God would be in more of a mess than I would. But over the subsequent months, God proved that that trustworthiness is real. Indeed, I have to say that the way God proved trustworthy over the sixteen months after we moved went far beyond my dreams. We had many little crises but none that God failed to take us through. Ann moved from "I don't want to go" to "It's better here than I expected" to "I like America more than England," and that is something I would not have dared pray for.

Halfway through the first term, one Tuesday in a time of informal worship, someone prayed that God would guard what God had written on our hearts. The next morning I wrote down some of those things:

- You love me like a protector with warmth and affection and steel.
- This is the right place for me, and it will be a place of refreshment.
- I am to give myself and will then find myself.
- You have given me the vocation of living with Ann's illness, and I accept it.

- You want me to prove that living with loss isn't incompatible with living with joy, and I enthusiastically accept that too.

At the beginning of the second term, I was asked to give a testimony in chapel, and I told people something of this story. At the end of the service a student came up to me and told me that during the worship part he had been given a picture of a man washing dishes, looking out over a garden, and of God saying, "I have heard you." As I spoke he knew the picture was for me. As we wept on each other's shoulders, I knew that this was not me here in Pasadena (where I wash dishes facing a wall!) but me in Nottingham, where I indeed washed dishes facing the garden with its fruit trees and birds and squirrels that Ann and I both loved. I knew that the picture was true, though only as I write do I realize its significance. I believed then that God was listening and that God would make things work out, but by the nature of the case, this had to be faith not sight. Now it was sight, and God was once again saying (in love, not in rebuke), "Do you see? I was listening, wasn't I?"

Of course, I am still working to trust God for the long-term issues. Trusting does not have an end—even in heaven. It is one of the three things that remain (see 1 Cor. 13:13).

19

Turbulence

In the late 1960s, we used to watch *Rowan and Martin Laugh-In*—I think it was on late Sunday nights, just right for an unwinding pastor. It proclaimed with pride that it came from beautiful Downtown Burbank. I could tell this was a joke, but now I live just along the freeway from the studios and appreciate more fully the irony of associating "beautiful" with Burbank. One of its regular items carried the tag line, "What do you want first, the good news or the bad news?"

The turbulence of our life has alternated between the two. Here are one week's recollections.

- Ann has an infection—we had better transfer her to the hospital.
- But she should be there only two or three days.
- After that, shouldn't you really put her in a nursing home?
- But if you want to keep her at home, we can offer you more support there.
- She has pneumonia.

- Her temperature is down today.
- Would you want us to resuscitate her if her heart stops?
- She is doing better—we can transfer her from the acute ward to the Transitional Care Unit.
- Her temperature is up again.
- Her temperature is down again.
- She ought to go to a skilled nursing facility after she's released from the hospital.
- But she should be able to come home after that.
- You shouldn't assume she will ever recover—should her sons come to say good-bye?
- There's no need for her to go to a skilled nursing facility—we can send a nurse to your home.
- Her temperature is up again.
- She can go home tomorrow.
- We've found out why her temperature has been going up—she has more fluid in her lungs.
- But the antibiotics should solve that—it just may take a bit longer.

Someone said that uncertainty is difficult. It's not quite that. The roller coaster is difficult.

The Last One Hundred Days?

In the last fall of the old millennium, I began to wonder whether Ann was dying. When we visited California in connection with the possibility of moving here, she could still get across a room with the help of a walker. During that visit, when we looked at the condo that seemed designed for us (and where I saw God's hand confirming this), there seemed only one thing unfitting about it: It had long-pile carpet that Ann would never be able to negotiate. But by the time we moved, she could not walk at all, and this became irrelevant.

In the fall, she lost the ability to lift a sandwich to her mouth. She found it more and more difficult to swallow. No matter how long she chewed, her swallowing reflex would fail to operate. Indeed, a spitting reflex sometimes came into play instead, with amusing if messy results. She had trouble taking her medicines, and she was not drinking near enough liquids. She stopped drinking coffee, one of her great delights. She was not getting enough nutrition. I could feed her continuously from 5:00 P.M. to 10:00 P.M., but she could sit for ten or twenty minutes chewing the same mouthful of food. She was visibly losing weight.

She found thinking and remembering more difficult, and she was talking less. Eventually, she reached a point when she hardly talked at all. If we got a yes or no out of her three times in a day, we were doing well.

Worse, sometimes she would look vague, or she would look past us as if not seeing us. She seemed to be losing control of her smile, the last physical movement she did control, though she still managed a slight response to a child or a cat or a hyacinth or a familiar face. Her head would shake from side to side. Sometimes she would drop off to sleep in the middle of a meal. Sometimes she would cry out inarticulately, and I did not know whether this was because she was in pain or because she wanted to clear her throat and could not do so or because she was frustrated that she could not formulate something to articulate. Whatever it was, I could do nothing about it.

And I began to wonder whether she was dying. Obviously, I knew that eventually she would die, but until this time I had assumed she might go on living as a disabled person for years. Although it had been painful watching her lose her freedom and her capacities and her mobility, we enjoyed our life together. Indeed, I found it hard to imagine things being any other way (as I found it hard to remember how they had been when she was not so reduced by the illness). While she grieved over the loss of the ability to work as a psychiatrist and to do things for herself, she was reasonably content. She was loved and well looked after by two caregivers who were with her for much of the day, especially when I was at work. She had been used to appreciating simple things such as eating ice cream by the pool and watching the birds and laughing at the British comedy *Keeping up Appearances,* and she enjoyed visits from students who came to our condo. I had been able to imagine that continuing for years.

Suddenly it was harder to imagine. The progress of the illness had all but taken away those remaining aspects of life that gave life some enjoyment, and it seemed that she was fading away and was not likely to survive much longer. I had never really understood what it was that people with MS die of, but I began to realize that it was what people die of in old age. They may catch some infection from which they fail to recover, or they may simply fade away and die. A friend in Britain with MS had died a few months previously. She had simply died in her sleep. I began to listen for Ann's breathing in the night and to wonder each morning when I got up whether she would still be alive.

One of the results of getting insufficient nourishment is that your skin begins to break down, and Ann had increasing trouble with pressure sores. One on her bottom refused to heal. Indeed, sitting for long periods of time trying to eat meant it got worse rather than better. At times during the day I would lay her on her side on the sofa to relieve the pressure. I could not see how we could go to a movie or on other outings without it getting worse. I gave away our tickets to a concert by the great blues artist Keb Mo. I began to spend the evenings sitting on the carpet by the sofa, just to be with Ann, thinking that a day would come when I would look back on these weeks as the last weeks of her life.

One afternoon she had a little seizure, the first she had had for several years. Her eyes flickered in odd ways, and her face distorted. Afterward, she was able to talk and swallow a bit, as if the seizure had shaken her system into functioning again. This lasted only a few days, but it seemed precious, a gift of God's grace. Those days would have been a good time to say good-bye, though we did not exactly do that, and later I realized that it was too late to have an actual conversation about her dying—a conversation in which she took part.

One day the nurse came to change Ann's catheter. She routinely took Ann's blood pressure, pulse, and so on. Ann's blood pressure was 240 over 120—twice the normal. She told us to go straight to the ER. Oddly, there Ann's blood pressure was 60 over something that did not register—half the normal but just as worrying. The problem was that she was dehydrated and consequently also deoxygenated. They put her on oxygen and a

saline IV, and after a couple of hours her blood pressure returned
to normal.

The doctor asked what they were to do if one day she stopped
breathing. How "aggressive" did I want them to be in seeking to
bring her back to life? This was not something they expected to
arise today, now that she was getting treatment for her low blood
pressure, but it might arise one day, and they would need to
know the answer. It was something I needed to talk to Ann about.
What would she want? I wept, partly because the idea of talking to her about the question seemed daunting. The doctor and
the nurse we often met there comforted me and commented on
how well looked after they thought Ann was.

When the nurse had told me to get Ann to the ER quickly, I
had simply done so, without a sense of panic. The sequence of
events reminded me of an occasion two months before when
she had fallen out of her wheelchair just outside our condo.
Unable to reach out to break her fall, she had hit her head on
the concrete, and blood had gushed out. At the time I was quite
cool in handling the situation, though again I wept in the hospital, and over the next few days the awfulness of the event kept
coming home. I kept seeing Ann falling. I kept reliving that split
second when she was on her way from wheelchair to concrete
and there was no time to get around to catch her. I kept feeling
the thud as her head hit the ground (and marveling that no more
damage was done). This time as I sat by her bed, I reflected on
the strangeness of waiting to discover whether they can pluck
your wife back from death and on the strangeness of not being
a panicky person.

We were two months away from the end of the millennium,
and we were looking forward to a visit from our two sons and
their wives and our grandson, whom Ann had not seen. I began
to wonder whether Ann would even live that long, though in less
gloomy moments I imagined she would do so, and I was
extremely grateful that we were to have this time together. A
year or so before, as we had sat in an outdoor restaurant near
our condo, one of our daughters-in-law had suddenly declared,
"This is where I wish to see in the new millennium," and had
gone off to reserve a table for ten. That was how it had come
about that we were all to be together. I could not imagine Ann

living another year, so it was great that we would have what I thought would be this last time of celebration together.

That November, Ann's neurologist decided to give Ann a course of steroids, a variant on the treatment that used to work well at earlier stages of the illness. During the second treatment, she began talking again and talked all day. It was another gift of grace. Then, within hours of finishing the course, she was back to where she had been before it. She could not take the steroids on a regular basis, and only occasionally again could she signify yes or no. Once or twice a day she uttered a clause.

I began to think in terms of these being the last one hundred days. It was a figure of speech. Although I felt that Ann was fading faster than she had done before, I had no idea how long the literal time frame would be. When we celebrated her birthday in November, I could not imagine ever doing so again. I began to think about her funeral. There should be pictures of her there, not least for people who did not know her when she was more alive. We should play the Beatles' "All My Loving," which she used to sing when she was a student, when she went to see if there was a letter from me. The van Gogh sunflowers, her favorite painting, should be there. And afterward, I would like to scatter her ashes in Dovedale in the Derbyshire Dales in England, where we began our honeymoon.

That evening I started the medication routine at 10:00 and found she could not swallow at all. I would put things in her mouth, and they would just stay there. But she was still alert—she knew what was going on. So I told her that I wondered if she was dying and that I was sorry we had not talked about dying and funerals, and I told her what I was thinking about for her funeral. I think she smiled slightly when I included the Beatles. She was then able to swallow.

Then we saw a gastroenterologist who agreed to fix Ann with a gastric feeding tube, but it would be weeks before he could do so. That afternoon, lunch dribbled out of Ann's mouth from 2:30 until 7:00. Then at 10:00 she started swallowing and took one can of nutrition and started talking, so we talked until 12:00. (She even asked for a drink of water in bed.) A day or two later, the gastroenterologist found Ann an appointment the next day instead of in mid-December. The inserting of the tube was as straightforward as they said it would be, and as soon as she began to get proper nutrition she began to do better, and the sores started to heal. It was like the postponement of an execution.

Admittedly, from time to time I continued to wonder whether she had died. I did so the next month, the morning one of our sons was due to arrive from England with his wife and baby. Perhaps Ann was not breathing when I got up, and I did not notice. If she is dead, what will we do today? They must be above Iceland now, with Daniel fulfilling Steven's nightmares, crawling up and down the aisle, and Steven himself has a nasty cold. . . . Should we send someone to meet them at the airport, to tell them? Could we keep Ann's body here all day until they arrive? Is that legal? What do you do when someone dies anyway? There seems little point in calling 911.

Then she cried out and coughed. So she was alive.

About this time I was invited to join a group of faculty and chaplains working through the Ignatian Spiritual Exercises. It felt like a gift from God at this turbulent stage in my life, something that would give me a fresh framework within which to cope with Ann's illness and decline. What follows in this chapter comes from my journaling of the process.

John 4:1–14

From somewhere I have in my head the words "not merely to survive but to triumph." I think they were a promise from God, and much of the time Ann and I have done the second and not merely the first. But here is a story about Jesus being apprehensive or pressured, sitting down wearily by a well, being hungry and thirsty, being alone and asking for refreshment, and through it I realized anew that it is okay to do and be those things.

Somehow the grief at Ann's inability to talk had that effect. It made me feel apprehensive. Every time I notice a new little loss, like the way her fingers and hands and wrists are now inclined to curl in as if she is folding in on herself, I think there cannot be any other way in which she loses, but she keeps finding new little ways, and each one is like a little death. I have become apprehensive about where it may lead. I have always thought I would be able to look after her till the end. But will I be able to? Just before we left England, I asked our physician how the future might turn out. In reality, I knew what his answer would be—that there is no way of telling. I did not guess that he would go on to say that on the basis of cases he knew I ought to come to terms with the fact that I would not always be able to look after her. Eventually, she would have to live in a nursing home. That would be terrible—worse than dying in a way. I couldn't imagine not being able to live together.

But the person who is tired and asks for help is the person who has an independent and unique source of fresh, running water and goes on to share it. Jesus shows supernatural resources, not natural resources that will run out. He makes a promise to the woman at the well that I know he has fulfilled for me and in a paradoxical way for Ann too. People who drink of his water find it transformed into their own fresh spring. I presume it then gushes up, not merely to give them life but to give life to other people—because that is what his spring is like. The fact that Ann brings life to other people is my evidence that Jesus has fulfilled the promise for her, even though often it does not look like it. So how do I share the spring that Jesus has set within me? The same way she does, I guess, just by "being." And by talking about it, and talking about Ann, especially since she cannot. And by being willing to show when I am tired or grieved or saddened by loss and potential loss, and in the way I show it by showing that I am also resourced. I am fortunate that I do not have an option about whether I reveal or conceal my feelings, joyful or grieved—they spill out!

Mark 9:14–29

There are disturbing similarities between Ann and the boy whom the disciples cannot heal while Jesus is away being transfigured in the company of the three leading disciples. The story concerns someone who has been ill for years, who is unable to speak. The person to whom he means so much and on whom he is utterly dependent has brought him to Jesus' disciples, but they can do nothing. Ann, too, has a spirit that prevents her from speaking. Food dribbles out of her mouth too. She can chew incessantly on her own saliva. She cannot drink, so she gets dehydrated and deoxygenated and falls asleep with food in her mouth. She, too, would fall over if I did not hold her up, or she goes mysteriously rigid.

The theologians have been on our side, oh yes, they have. We have lived among theologians for thirty years, and they have loved us and prayed with us and grieved with us and puzzled with us and never ever spoken harsh words to us. But for us Jesus does not come back from the mountain. He stays in heaven transfigured. He knows what is going on but does nothing— nothing by way of confronting this spirit of incapacity and dumbness.

It arouses some challenges from me. I want to answer Jesus back when he addresses the disciples or the crowd or the theologians or the victim of the illness and calls them a faithless generation with whom he does not wish to spend more time than is absolutely necessary. I want to answer him back when he reiterates the father's words: "If you are able." It does not seem an unreasonable phrase. Jesus seems so hard. I want to say, "If you are able, let's have some pity and some support instead of this aggressiveness. I believe you have the power, so how about using it?"

I want to answer him back when he suggests that people will be healed if we pray. It is but one of the gaps and illogicalities in the story—after all, the passage does not say that Jesus prayed. Maybe that is a parable of how little we know. And the whole story is reminiscent of God's speech in Job, reminding Job that he is not the center of the universe and that he is not going to be told the answers to his questions. Like Job, the man and his son are just minor players in a drama, one involving Jesus and the disciples and the scribes and the evil powers. And so Ann and I are just minor players in a drama. And perhaps this helps me to see where comfort lies in the story.

The comfort is that the way in which God reaches out to you may vary according to your place in the drama, but God does reach out to you. God did that with people who had a very tough time, such as Job or Saul, and he does it with this man and his son, and he does it with Ann and me. Everybody gets used, but only in a way that will also bring some meaning and some consolation to them somehow.

I want to ask Mark some questions, as well as Jesus. Why did you tell us stories like this, about someone being healed, when you know that in most other people's lives sick people do not get healed? Would it not be better if we did not have these stories?

At the end of a meditation we are supposed to talk to God, but I want to do that with anger, not with love and reverence. I ask God, "What do you say back?" and receive at least a sense that it is okay to have said what I did, and an awareness that somehow one can live with a story like this.

Luke 13:10–17

"Should not this woman, a daughter of Abraham, whom Satan has kept bound for eighteen long years, be set free on the Sabbath day from what bound her?" (v. 16). "Jesus wants to heal anyone who suffers. He does not let established custom hinder God's healing gift," said the notes that accompany the meditation.

Huh! I know a woman afflicted for eighteen years—more, actually. You do not want to heal her, do you? *Do you?* Do you grieve over her, without healing her? There are no stories about that. There are promises of that day when tears of pain get wiped away. In the meantime, you are tough-minded in resolutely not healing.

Where is this woman's husband or father? What will he make of it? His life is being turned upside down. If Ann were healed, I wouldn't know how to start living. But I would soon find out! I would have to stop being in charge. But that would be nice. I would not have to be self-sufficient. All those constraints would disappear—being out for only a few hours at a time, having to have sitters here. She would welcome me home. I would explain things and she would understand.

What does the woman think? She was not looking to be healed. She did not ask. She was glad, though. Jesus interferes in our lives unasked to do things that have nothing to do with us—you wanted your Father to be glorified and you wanted to put the theologians in their place. It is pure chance whether we

are in the way when you want to do something. You want to do
something with us too, but it is through not healing. You want
to prove something to people—that joy is still possible, that
courage stays possible, that it is possible to carry on caring, that
you can summon up those resources from within us by the Holy
Spirit, that happiness does not lie in what we can do or how far
we can travel or how wealthy we are.

I have often said that I can no longer pray for healing for Ann,
though I am happy for other people to do so. But at the same
time I am not prepared to ask for Ann to be set free by death. It
is not because I do not believe in God or in resurrection and
therefore doubt whether she would find real relief in going to
be with Jesus. It is not because I am afraid to face being without her. I am afraid of that, but I am ready to face it when the
time comes.

I think I now know what it is. I cannot raise the spiritual
energy to have God say no again. But there is something else.
To ask God to take Ann and release her (and me!) is to ask for
God to change our vocation, to ask God to stop working through
us in the way God does. And I do not want to do that.

A friend who has to live with an ongoing grief and loss like
ours once said that he looked at us and said, "Well, if John and
Ann can do it, maybe I can." It's not just a matter of *whether* but
how. Once we had students over for pizza after class, and one
of them—an interesting, edgy woman who often looks and talks
as if she lives with tensions and anger—commented on the way
I am usually upbeat despite Ann's illness. Don't I ever feel loss?
I explained that of course I do but that I had decided long ago
that I (we) were going to enjoy life. We would have to work
within the constraints of the illness, but accepting those, we
would have a good time. To put it another way, I decided we
would not be beaten by the illness.

One day I imagine God will decide that enough is enough and
will free Ann and will bring our turbulence to an end. But for
now I am content. In a strange way, that means Jesus' phrase
does not apply to Ann. She isn't really bound by Satan, because
what might have been Satan's bonds have been turned into Jesus'
freedom.

20

Vocation

In the Midst of Life We Are in Death (and Vice Versa)

I carry with me the image of Ann and Daniel, our grandson, sitting alongside each other in the kitchen. Ann is in her wheelchair, Daniel in his highchair. Both need to be lifted there and fed there. Both are helpless without the assistance of the rest of us. I had met Daniel briefly when he was two weeks old, but the person who arrived for a visit at the turn of the millennium was a bouncing fifteen-month-old, full of life and energy. One great wonder of the time was the joy he brought to Ann. She talked and smiled and laughed whenever he was about. The talk was still just phrases such as "Where's the baby?" but that was more than usual.

Daniel is full of dynamic energy, waving his arms and his feet, banging on his table, having a go at feeding himself, shouting, grinning, looking round. His dynamism and energy highlights Ann's loss of these. Although occasionally she will smile or groan, her slight movements of head or hands are involuntary. She and

Daniel are passing each other on the train tracks that join life and death, traveling in opposite directions.

In T. S. Eliot's poem about the Magi's visit to see Jesus, the Magi describe their visit as an experience of death and not just of life. The motif is not present in the actual story in Matthew, though it *is* present in the story in Luke 2 when Jesus is presented to God in the temple forty days after his birth, in keeping with the instructions in Leviticus 12.

The time comes for "their" purification. "They" are presumably Mary and Jesus, and it may seem odd that either should need purification at this moment. The church's readings for the Feast of the Presentation encourage us to think that this purification has something to do with sin. But the stain and cleansing that are involved in birth do not relate to sin. They are similar to the stain and cleansing attached to menstruation or the emission of semen or to other forms of contact with blood or with bodily emissions or with death. They reflect an awareness of being in contact with something mystical, mysterious, awesome, numinous. We are in touch with matters of life and death. We thought that life and death were different things, Eliot's Magi comment, but we found that they were interwoven. In the Old Testament, some effort was thus made to keep life and death separate. People were not supposed to cook a kid goat in its mother's milk, for instance, which brings life and death into harsh juxtaposition. People were encouraged to be awed by menstrual blood, which strangely holds together death (blood) and life (the possibility of conception). Israel knew that life and death were different yet interwoven.

Birth itself makes that especially clear, for by its nature it involves blood, which threatens death. Birth can often mean the death of the mother and/or the child. Just recently we saw the film *The Songcatcher,* set in the Appalachians in the early part of the twentieth century, which incorporated more than one example of such death being threat or actuality. Even today, a hospital put up a notice reminding staff that the first ten minutes of a person's life are among the most dangerous; someone added that the last ten minutes could be pretty tricky too. Giving birth and being born are matters of life and death, moments when we are in touch with mysterious, supernatural realities and are virtually unable to avoid transgressing the fine line between them. The rite of purification reestablished that line, but in doing so it reaffirmed its thinness. Life and death are interwoven.

The birth of a firstborn son took parents and son near that line in a different way. Life belonged to God and came from God. The Israelites recognized this by giving the first of the crops and the firstborn of animals back to God. For them, life became death. God did not require this actual offering of human offspring, but he did require a firstborn son to be formally and sacramentally presented to God and to have an offering made in his place in recognition of this debt. Life could have meant death for him were it not for God's desire to receive a symbolic offering in his place.

So much was true of any firstborn that day in Jerusalem. There is more to be said about Jesus. A man called Simeon awaits his arrival. We assume he is an old man, though the story does not say so. But it does say he is a man with death on his mind. God has told him he will not see death until he has seen the Lord's Messiah. Jesus' birth means his death, and that is fine by him, because he has seen all that he ever wanted to see.

Simeon affirms that in a way all this applies to others as well. "This child is destined for the falling and the rising of many in Israel." It will begin with the death of the babies in Bethlehem, and it will end with the mysterious rising of corpses from tombs at the moment of Jesus' own death. Jesus' act of taking up his cross will demand of anyone who follows him that they do the same. Paradoxically, they will then discover that they gain their lives rather than losing them. Death and life are interwoven. "A sword will pierce your own soul too," he adds to Mary. Life will mean death for her.

Finally, there appears a prophet called Anna. She is a woman of great age, a woman whose vigorous life of worship, fasting, and prayer belies the proximity to death that her years suggest. In spirit, she is fully alive, even if her body is near death. In her own way, she, too, belies the distinction between life and death.

Perhaps Anna and Simeon stand for the worship of the temple as a whole. It is full of life and vitality and meaning, but it is destined soon to die because of the different life and vitality and meaning embodied in this new life that Mary and Joseph have brought to present to God. Leaving the presence of the about-to-die Simeon and the aged Anna, Joseph and Mary take Jesus to a new home where he grows and becomes strong and is filled with wisdom.

Yes, death and life are interwoven. My daughter-in-law's willingness to risk death meant life for Daniel. Daniel's liveliness calls forth life from Ann. Ann's dying brings both dying and life to me. It calls forth life from people she meets, even as it invites them to face weakness and death. One day we sat in a cafe. For a while Ann was able to swallow, and I fed her pieces of chocolate truffle and spoonfuls of tea. After a while a woman walked up and said it had been a blessing to her just to watch. There had been something life-giving about Ann's dying.

Dying

There have been three occasions when I thought Ann was dying. Admittedly, once every few days I wonder momentarily whether she has actually died. Usually it is when she seems very quiet in bed, and I look to see whether she stopped breathing in the night. I guess that one day she may die in the night like that— indeed, I rather hope so, because most of the alternative ways of dying are grimmer.

But on three occasions I have thought she was soon going to die. The first was when she had her convulsive seizure. In reality, it was not life-threatening, but in the middle of the night when you have never seen such convulsions before, it seemed so. The second was when she lost the ability to swallow. That was a genuinely life-threatening development.

Then a few weeks ago she developed pneumonia. With hindsight, I should have spotted it some while before it became a crisis. She had been coughing and spluttering for a week or two, and I had propped up the top of her bed on a concrete block to try to discourage the coughing and spluttering during the night so that she (and I!) could get some sleep. She had also been moaning and groaning. One Friday we went to see *Citizen Kane*. Twice I had to bring her out of the auditorium because I was afraid she was disturbing other people with noises that were not merely disputing the claim that this is the greatest movie ever made. On that Sunday she was groaning again and looking very hot, and I would probably have taken her to the ER were it not for the fact that a nurse was due to visit the next morning. The nurse came, took one look at her (or rather, found that her temperature was 103.6 and her pulse 150), and said "Get her to the ER straightaway." They put her on an IV and worked to get her temperature down and that evening transferred her to the hospital.

The discovery of antibiotics means that having pneumonia is not usually life-threatening for an otherwise healthy person, but I knew that it is one of the ways that people with MS die, as is the case with elderly people. Their internal weaknesses mean they may no longer be able to cough up phlegm or swallow their saliva properly, and neither can they stop such material eventually drifting back into their lungs. Infection follows, and they cannot fight it as effectively as other people can. But the antibiotics did the fighting for Ann, and she was home before the week was out.

A few weeks later, however, she again spent a night coughing and spluttering, and it seemed as if the pneumonia might be returning. Near midnight that night one of our sons phoned to tell us that his wife had just had a baby girl, our first granddaughter, and once more I thought about the strange way life and death interweave. In the morning, when things often look a little less gloomy than they do in the small hours as you toss and turn, I sat with God and found myself saying, "I know Ann will be all right. She will be with you. And I know I will be all right."

The next day doctors took X rays and did tests and eventually concluded that Ann had two or three different, smaller problems but that the pneumonia had not returned. Over the next few days, the action they took would solve one problem but would also cause another as a side effect, and so on. . . .

At about that time, someone commented to me that it must be wearing to go through a bereavement that takes years to happen. If we could know that Ann would live for two weeks or two months or two years, I could get on with handling that. The wearing thing is the roller-coaster nature of the process, anticipating the death that never comes, resolving one problem that is then succeeded by another. Actually, I do not really believe

she will ever die—she will just go on dying forever. I think of her
life and death in terms of the curve on a differential calculus
graph that keeps getting ever nearer the baseline but takes infin-
ity to get there. You keep thinking it must reach it, yet by definition it never does so. I have noted that it often seems there is
nothing left to happen, that Ann has nothing left to lose—then
something else happens, and she loses something else. But she
has been dying for so long that I cannot imagine her dying.

Keeping Alive

How long are we going to keep Ann alive? That has been the
gist of a question raised with me a number of times over the past
two years by doctors, therapists, and chaplains.

I could see that one could ask such a question about Tony
Bland, the teenager who was crushed at a British soccer game
and was in a vegetable state, but it had not occurred to me that
the same question concerned Ann. Thinking about it, I realize
that there are closer parallels than I might have cared to
acknowledge. We feed Ann through a tube, and we drain her
urine through another tube. We give her various forms of medicine to enable her to evacuate her bowels and sometimes have
to intervene in other ways to make that happen. We put pillows
in strategic places and move her from time to time to avoid the
occurrence of pressure sores. We exercise her unmoving fingers
and hands and elbows. I listened to some lectures on caring for
people with Alzheimer's, and the lecturer argued strongly against
the use of a gastric feeding tube. It prolongs a life that it is inappropriate to prolong. In Ann's case, did we prolong a life when
it was inappropriate to do so?

In the United States, Australian ethicist Peter Singer is the
great advocate of *Rethinking Life and Death,* the title of a book
whose jacket locates it "in the tradition of Aldous Huxley's *Brave
New World.*" He is enough of a media celebrity to have made an
appearance on Charlie Rose's nightly interview program on pub-
lic television. A recent issue of the American Jewish monthly
Commentary carried an advertisement for a book by Wesley J.
Smith called *The Culture of Death: The Assault on Medical Ethics*

in America. According to the advertisement, the book shows how "the 'right to die' is slowly being transformed into the duty to die."

In the hospital last month, I was struck by the matter-of-fact way in which a charge-nurse placed under my nose a form that indicated which types of action I wanted taken if Ann's death seemed to be imminent. Do you want resuscitation? Yes or no? Do you want use of a respirator/ventilator? Yes or no? Do you want blood transfusion? Yes or no? And so on. I felt like a wimp answering yes to them all.

The doctors, therapists, chaplains, and Singer are not inventing a problem, and they are certainly not heartless people. Indeed, in a review article about Singer's work in the *New Republic*, with the subtitle "Other People's Mothers," Peter Berkowitz contrasted Singer's published views with his treatment of his own mother, who apparently has Alzheimer's. Singer sees that she is well looked after, Berkowitz pointed out, and rightly, though he thus "flagrantly violates" his own moral theory.[1] "It is different when it's your mother," Singer comments, according to Michael Spector's earlier profile of "The Dangerous Philosopher" in the *New Yorker*.[2] It is another way of noting the contrast between the professional and the layperson. Even the professional is a layperson in other contexts. I myself, of course, write as another version of this combination. Singer acknowledges that when you are personally involved, it makes you realize that "perhaps it is more difficult than I thought before."[3]

I am continually moved by the loving stance that people in the caring professions take to Ann and me and by the energy and skill of their caring. They are faced with the downside of the extraordinary technological advances that make it more and more possible to prolong a life that has no "quality." I can see that Ann's life can seem that way. She has tubes sticking out of different orifices. The only part of her body that she seems to have control over are her eyebrows, which I have often given her cause to raise. She cannot move a finger. If I hold her hand, I get no response. She can rarely even smile, except when I tickle the side of her mouth, and I sometimes wonder if that is involuntary. She has virtually no sensation in her body. Unknown to both of us, her hand once slipped down onto the wheel of her wheelchair when we were out walking, and it was raw and bleeding by the time we reached our destination—which was, happily, the doctor's office. She does not know what country she lives in, or what city, let alone what day it is, nor would she be sure of the names of any of the people she ever sees except me (I think/hope).

So the next time she catches pneumonia, as she will, should we really take her into the hospital and put her on an IV and fill her full of antibiotics and hope this is not the occasion when they cease to be effective or when her system stops fighting? Or should we follow the doctor's invitation and opt for hospice care, which ensures someone is comfortable and free of pain while they die a natural death in the context of their family and loved ones?

It is notoriously difficult to define the moment of death, and this is in strange harmony with the Israelite awareness of the mysterious overlap between life and death. Earlier I noted how the overlap appears in the Psalms, which are inclined to speak of so-called life as if it were death ("I was in the depths of Sheol"). They imply it is possible to be overcome by death while you are still alive. I have come to believe that people in the Old Testament looked for symbolic ways of affirming the real distinction between life and death because they recognized that life and death actually overlap. They do in Ann's case. Are we insisting on holding on to Ann when she and God both think it is time for her to go?

Vocation and Loss

The trouble is that the professionals' stance differs so much from the layperson's. The professionals' stance matches fears of my own that I have hardly articulated. It can seem now as if Ann is almost gone—gone to be with Jesus, gone to rest in Abraham's bosom. There is so little of her here now. In her disability, Ann exercised her ministry to people, even though I have a hard time discerning the mystery of what this ministry was or how it worked. But much of the time she exercised this ministry when she could communicate a bit, at least by responding with a smile to people who said hello. She can hardly exercise it now, can she?

I voiced that suspicion to one of the people who comes to sit with Ann from time to time—doing so not because we need her to but because she wants to. She has known Ann for only a year and has therefore no acquaintance with Ann when she was more responsive. "No," she protested. "Ann's spirit ministers to my spirit." We have another friend who sits with Ann and reads to her. She says she leaves healed and human—something she does not feel when she deals with fully functioning people the rest of the week.

Ann lost the ability to speak at about the same time she lost the ability to swallow, and the comment about her spirit reminded me of the words of another friend. Ann's problem with speaking is not a physical one, so that we could provide her with another means of expressing herself. It is a neurological problem affecting the brain itself, and it means she cannot work out what she wants to say. A speech therapist explained to me that "encoding" (working out what you want to say) is four times more difficult than "decoding" (working out what someone else has said to you). Ann can understand much of what people say and much of what goes on, but receiving information is a much simpler process than formulating a response, which she cannot do. I had expressed my fear that Ann's inability to work out what to say meant she could not be relating to God, because she could not articulate things to God. Our friend pointed out that God's spirit and Ann's spirit could be in communication even if her brain were not involved. I have come to realize that of course she and I relate to each other even though she has hardly any more means of communicating with me in a traditional sense than she has with anyone else.

Three months ago I was giving Bible expositions at a meeting of the Lausanne Consultation on Jewish Evangelism in Los Angeles. I was talking about Moses and his extraordinary freedom in talking with God and about the way he provokes God into responding. "It's never worked for me," a friendly heckler interrupted. That led me to describe some of the ways I have talked to God about Ann, which led a woman to ask to talk with me. She had just discovered that she had MS, and she wondered what this was going to mean for her and her husband. He was about to fly off for three months to teach on another continent, and that was typical of the ministry he exercised. I found myself telling this woman that I had come to realize that looking after Ann was my vocation. I am not sure I had ever articulated it that way to someone before.

One neat thing about a vocation is that you probably don't mind fulfilling it. I can see why people can be tempted to admire the way I look after Ann, but there are several reasons why they should resist the temptation. One is that they do not see the ways in which I have failed her over the years. Another reason is that looking after Ann is not a nasty task. As I have implied, people like being with Ann and somehow get something out of it, and I like being with her too.

It is hard to know how things are for Ann herself now, but I know how things were a year or two ago when she was more articulate. She had long felt a deep loss at not being able to do more, in particular, not being able to work as a psychiatrist as she once did. Yet generally she had a kind of contentment about her, and I think she still has that. In this sense, she has looked happier in recent years than when she was much fitter, when she was a more driven and worrying person. One of her care-givers comments that Ann accepts anything as it is.

> Ann's acceptance led me to be able to accept myself and to be myself. In Ann I found peace and a resting place and God's acceptance of every human being. In my four years with Ann, I have never heard her shout or grumble or say something bad to someone. Once when we had waited several hours for a handicapped taxi and I was feeling impatient at the service we were receiving, she simply said, "Take it easy, Yanti." In Ann, Jesus' life became real to me.

Of course, sensing a vocation does not neutralize an awareness of catastrophic loss. When Daniel and his parents came to stay with us, it was as if we were watching ourselves thirty years ago. I knew it moved me and disturbed me in some way, though I did not know quite why. The experience came to a climax as we said good-bye and they put Daniel into the car and stowed the last pieces of luggage and sat beside each other in the front and drove off. I went back into our condo and burst into tears.

Only the next day did I work out why. In looking at them, I was seeing Ann and me thirty years ago, and I was thrust into an awareness of the fact that we had lost so much over thirty years. Once we lived and worked together as parents and spouses and friends and lovers as these two do, and now we do not, and I had forgotten what it was like. Suddenly, I experienced this huge sense of loss at what Ann's illness has taken away from us.

It has been fifteen or twenty years since we were a regular married couple, and my memory is dominated by the subsequent years of progressive weakening. Sometimes I look at old photographs, or even photographs from three or four years ago, and I am again overwhelmed by the sense of loss. Or I will see a married couple and be overwhelmed by a sense of shock that this is how we once were and might have been. Or I will come across letters from nearly forty years ago and be stupefied at the liveliness of the person who wrote them.

But I do not usually think about such things. For better and for worse, I am a person who lives in the present, and I am not very good at regrets about the past or worries about the future. That instinct to live in the present makes me get on with enjoying life with Ann as it is. There is nothing wrong with looking after someone. It is an enjoyable, human thing to do, like cooking or making things grow or knitting—or like being a pastor or a theologian or a writer or a teacher, my other vocations.

Since articulating the conviction that looking after Ann is my vocation, I have come to see that this suggests a way of looking at Ann's illness itself, and I am trying to think about the question of "keeping her alive" in the light of it. Ann would be several times dead were it not for the wonders of medicine, but the continuing development of these extraordinary ways of keeping people alive means we have a pressing need to discern when to use them. So we talk about the sanctity of life. Or we talk about quality of life or about what is best for a patient and the family. Or we ask whether the expenditure involved is justified. Or we ask about the number of others whose lives could be saved if we would let this person die and use his or her organs for transplants.

In a postmodern context, we need hardly look for a single criterion in making decisions about life and death. What I want to do here is suggest another criterion that might provide a clue for discerning God's will in a situation such as this. Over the years, as she has had to live with her increasing disability, Ann has had a vocation to minister to people out of that experience. The question is, Does she still have that vocation? I do not imply that this question is any easier to answer than the other questions. For Ann, in some obvious ways, it might be far better to go to be with Christ than to stay here, but when Paul articulated that conviction about what was best for him, he added the recognition that his vocation was to stay to continue his ministry (Phil. 1:23–24). His ministry was not completed.

I do not know for certain whether God gave Ann a choice about whether she should let her disability become her vocation. But one reason for believing that God did so is that we faced some of these issues thirty-five years ago when her illness was diagnosed. I know she said yes to God then, without knowing what that yes might mean, as I did myself. Soon afterward, we both said yes to God when her neurologist recommended that she have an abortion because of the effect the pregnancy would have on her illness.

Another reason for believing that she has been willing to let her disability become her vocation is that it seems unlikely she would be able to exercise her apparently involuntary ministry now if in some sense she were not actually willing to do so. Her caregiver whom I quoted above speaks of once asking Ann how she dealt with MS and with her loss. Ann acknowledged that this was difficult at first, but she said she learned to live with it and to live by Paul's declaration that God makes everything work together for people who are called by God and love God (Rom. 8:28).

Willingly or not, she has a vocation. She has exercised a vocation to me, so that my fulfilling one in relation to her is only a reciprocation. She has exercised this vocation to other people and continues to do so. The question for the future, then, is whether she still has this vocation—whether she is still called to it.

Things were simpler in the days when we did not have the opportunity, as we do now, to control the destiny of another person. But for better or for worse, to some extent we now have this opportunity—beginning at the moment of birth or the first time we give a child antibiotics. We decide whether to keep that child alive or whether to let that child die. I hope I find Ann peacefully dead in bed before we have to think some more about that. But I am not banking on it.

Epilogue

When I was discussing with an editor the American edition of this book, he suggested that people would want to know what had happened since I wrote the first edition, when we were in the midst of our risky move to California. So I have brought our story up-to-date. The trouble is that anyone with such curiosity will still have the same reaction, because our story has not come to an end. In a sense, our human stories never do, except when we die. That is one of the reasons why we like novels and movies. They usually have endings ("closure"), and they reassure us that this may also be true of our own stories. Bible stories have little closure (look at Genesis–Kings or Mark or Acts, for instance), but they imply that their stories contain the promise of closure, even though they cannot know what that will look like. Our own unfinished stories are set in the context of those stories, and they share that promise. Ann's is and does, and mine is and does.

Notes

Chapter 4

1. Stanley Hauerwas, *Naming the Silences* (Grand Rapids: Eerdmans, 1990), 2.
2. Ibid., 53.
3. Stanley Hauerwas, *Suffering Presence* (Notre Dame, Ind.: University of Notre Dame Press, 1986), 77.
4. Ibid., 78.
5. Ibid., 77.
6. Ibid., 80.

Chapter 5

1. Roger Pooley and Philip Seddon, eds., *The Lord of the Journey* (San Francisco: Collins, 1986), 67; reprinted from *The Sermons of John Donne,* 10 vols. (Berkeley: University of California Press, 1953–62), vol. 6, 172.
2. John of the Cross, "The Ascent of Mount Carmel," book 1, chap. 13, in *The Collected Works of St. John of the Cross* (Washington, D.C.: ICS, 1991), 149–50.

Chapter 7

1. Steve Turner, *Hungry for Heaven,* rev. ed. (Downers Grove, Ill.: InterVarsity Press, 1995), 153.
2. Ibid.

Chapter 10

1. Dan Cohn-Sherbock, *Holocaust Theology* (London: Lamp Press, 1989).

Chapter 11

1. Hannah Hurnard, *Hinds' Feet on High Places* (London: Christian Literature Crusade, 1955), 16.
2. Ibid., 17.
3. Ibid.
4. Richard Olivier, *Shadow of the Stone Heart* (London: Pan, 1995), 160.
5. Ibid., 182.
6. Hurnard, *Hinds' Feet on High Places*, 115–16.

Chapter 16

1. Derek Kidner, *Genesis* (London: Tyndale; Downers Grove, Ill.: InterVarsity Press, 1967), on the passage.
2. John Stott, *The Message of Ephesians* (Downers Grove, Ill.: InterVarsity Press, 1979), on the passage.

Chapter 17

1. Maggie Ross, *The Fountain and the Furnace: The Way of Tears and of Fire* (New York: Paulist Press, 1987), 21–22, 29.
2. Ibid., 227.
3. Maggie Ross, *Pillars of Flame: Power, Priesthood, and Spiritual Maturity* (London: SCM, 1988), 38, author's emphasis.
4. Ibid., 124.
5. Ibid., xvii.
6. Ibid., xviii.
7. Cf. *The Collected Works of St. Teresa of Avila*, vol. 2 (Washington, D.C.: ICS, 1980), 317–18, 394–95.

Chapter 20

1. Peter Berkowitz, "The Utilitarian Horrors of Peter Singer: Other People's Mothers," *New Republic*, 10 January 2000.
2. Michael Spector, "The Dangerous Philosopher," *New Yorker*, 6 September 1999.
3. Ibid.